Fountains

in the Midst

Fountains
in the Midst

Cynthia Shomaker

XULON PRESS

Xulon Press
2301 Lucien Way #415
Maitland, FL 32751
407.339.4217
www.xulonpress.com

Printed in the United States of America

Paperback ISBN-13: 978-1-66282-974-1
Ebook ISBN-13: 978-1-66282-975-8

for my children...
great is His faithfulness

*"I will open up rivers in desolate heights,
and fountains in the midst of valleys;
I will make the wilderness a pool of water,
and the dry land springs of water."*
Isaiah 41:18

Fountains in the Midst

I've been praying about whether to record what I will share here for a long time. It's incredibly personal, and doubt has often lingered close at the very thought of putting into this format the things scribed on my heart.

The answer came in the most unexpected way.

I was washing dishes, just doing the daily routine of caring for my family, when a question dropped in my spirit that I knew was not my own thought process.

"You've never studied Habakkuk, have you?"
Well, no. Actually, I'm not sure I even know how to spell it correctly.

"Well, then. There you go."

So, to Habakkuk I went. I approached it in my usual way, researching and taking copious notes. The answer to my prayer, however, didn't show up in hours of study. It instead leapt like a lightning bolt into my spirit when I got to the second chapter.

> **"Write the vision and make it plain on**
> **tablets, that he may run who reads it."**
> **Habakkuk 2:2**

"The vision" is sharing the tenderness of the Lord given as I have daily sought His presence and Word. And, I had just purchased a new "tablet."

Well, then. There you go.

It's not about me and my doubt or fear at the thought of releasing the words given. It's about encouraging whoever will read them so they are *strengthened to run*. It's about sharing the comfort I've received so that others can be comforted themselves. It's about hope. Strength. Vision for restoration, when that seems like an impossible dream.

It's not about me.
It's about you hopefully hearing the echo of the Word in your own spirit and finding new joy in the Lord, which is—without a doubt—your great and matchless strength.

The Title...
As the idea of sharing this weighed heavy on my mind, I asked the Lord to put a title on my heart. Naming a study had always come quickly and easily,

but this time nothing seemed right. Nothing fit. I put the thought aside.

He gave it to me, once again seemingly out of the blue, as I was driving up the mountain one afternoon. I was listening to a CD of Scripture that a friend had given me, and as a man's voice read those powerful words, I was hit with the answer.

> *"I will open rivers in desolate heights, and **fountains in the midst** of valleys..." Isaiah 41:18.*

Those words leapt like fire in my bones, as they so accurately described what the Lord had done, and still does, for me. *He opened rivers of Himself to quench my dry, desolate, aching heart. He poured into my deep valley His fountain of mercy and grace, His beautiful words and presence.*

It was perfect.

Tender Mercies...
During a particularly difficult season of trials that stretched into years, I asked the Lord to show me daily some token of His tender mercy. *He's so faithful. He poured out rivers of grace and walked me through the darkness on the sheer mercy of His Words to me.* My tender mercies were scribbled down, stained with coffee and tears.

I give them to you.

I share these words in chronological order in the pattern they ministered to me. Mighty and awesome is the Lord Most High, Who moves through time and patterns and releases the divine into the mundane. *I pray Holy Spirit speaks to your deepest places and does a work He alone can do.* He's after your wholeness. He's bent on your healing. His love is beyond description, able to push back fear.

Be blessed.

The Words...

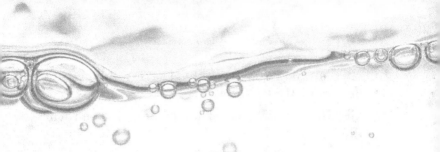

Coming To *Feast*

Oh, My beautiful hosts, come near.

Quiet your singing; look on in wonder.

My Child is coming to feast.

My Beloved is approaching My table,

and be assured, much awaits.

My table is spread with apples of gold in settings
of silver,

with Living Water, priestly oil

and sacred Bread.

I have spread My robe as its covering,

I have lifted My own hand and spoken deep blessing.

My Beloved thinks the blessing of the table will
be theirs,

and it most definitely will,

but there is a reciprocal blessing that thrills My heart.

My Spirit soars with the fellowship of My Bride.

My heart pounds with joy.

My soul finds great delight.

There is no good thing I withhold as this Child makes their way to My Presence.

I will pull back the Seat of Mercy and motion them to the seat of honor.

Their worship thrills Me,

and their fellowship causes My own song to pour out.

I rejoice over them;

My delight fills the earth.

All My blessing pours out on My seated ones, because I simply cannot resist.

They are My precious possession, My royal priests, the joy set before Me.

And as they step up to feast, My perfume soaks them, My splendor saturates

and their heartbeat becomes tuned to Mine.

So, heavenly hosts, quiet your sweet song—

My Beloved and I are going to feast.

> *"Behold, I stand at the door and knock. If anyone hears My voice and opens the door,*
> *I will come in to him and dine with him, and he with Me." Revelation 3:20*
>
> *The Lord your God in your midst, The Mighty One, will save;*
> *He will rejoice over you with gladness, He will quiet you with His love,*
> *He will rejoice over you with singing. Zephaniah 3:17*

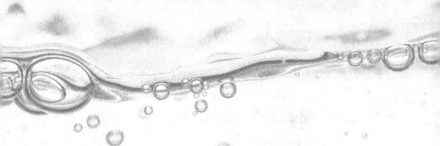

The Chair

The enemy has pulled back a chair and invited me to sit.

Years swirl in my head, weakness sets in, fatigue of body reaches heart.

And that chair looks awfully good.

Yet unseen labels rest on that seat that will jump into soul if you settle in...

Discouragement, Depression, Defeat, Dissolved Relationships, Despair, Deception....

That chair will strip you bare and steal every ounce of joy...

but it's padded, it looks so comfortable, there's a wide path leading to it

and I'm so tired.

Don't go. Don't take a step. Don't sit down.

Turn around and press into the only place of victory—*the Lord Jesus.*

Tell Him how your heart is wandering, wavering, weary.

3

Tell Him how much you'd love to sit down in that chair over there.

Ask Him what He has to say on the matter.

Ask Him to pour His Spirit into every weary, wounded place and heal, seal, strengthen,

establish on solid ground.

He has a chair waiting for you, too.

His has some labels on it, too.

It's called a throne, fashioned for a royal priesthood.

A seat of honor, crafted for a Bride.

A seat of mercy meant just for the weary and wounded like you.

A beautiful, delightful place whose labels are *Healing, Living, Established, Covered, Received, Accepted, Well-Loved, Beloved One, Cherished of Heaven.*

Sit here, Child.

The Father has a word for you.

You are not rejected or despised, forsaken or neglected.

Those things do not have a place in your heart.

You are My treasured Warrior, but some arrows have come your way.

I want to heal you.

I want you to sit in this place and enter My rest and, when I commission you to arise and shine, your healed feet will run with amazement.

You never have to leave the place of the Chair, because it is forever, and at all times,

available to you.

Sit and be strengthened. Sit and listen. Sit and be fed. Sit and receive healing.

Precious One, oh, precious Child, I know what tempts you to run to the enemy's chair.

I can handle it.

Sit in My seat of Mercy and keep bringing it to Me.

You are safe and secure. You are not alone, even when all around you have left.

Come, weary one, sit with Me awhile, and you will find lasting, glorious, restorative, true *REST.*

> "...and made us sit together in the heavenly places in Christ Jesus..."
> Ephesians 2:6b
>
> Be still and know that I am God...
> Psalm 46:10a

Fear Not

Fear is not fitting for a child of the Most High God.
Fear not, fear not, fear not—
for you, Beloved,
have power, love, and a sound mind infused with
wisdom, knowledge and revelation by
the breath of the Holy Spirit and
the activity of the living Word of God!
You encounter evil, but you are delivered.
You see trouble and tribulation,
but it does not overcome or overtake you,
because you are indwelt by the Spirit of the
One True God,
who defends you mightily and
crowns you more than a conqueror.

What is it exactly that you fear, Child?
Is there anything greater than Me?
Is fear not based on an inward or outward focus
rather than an *upward* one?

Where are your eyes?
Give them to Me.
Walk.
Step. Step. Step.
Come, Child, with Me.
You're not walking on your own.
I am holding you, steadying you,
moving the stones in front of you,
showing you the way.
I Myself uphold and deliver you.
You will not fail.

> *There is no fear in love; but perfect love casts out fear... 1 John 4:18*
>
> *For God has not given us a spirit of fear, but of power and of love and of a sound mind. 2 Timothy 1:7*

Timeless Praise

From everlasting to everlasting we are sheltered by the wing of the Most High,

and we can shout to the Ancient of Days with hearts full of time,

full of worship that reverberates through the ages and joins the chorus of every praise ever lifted.

A hymn of praise to the King,

the song of Moses and the song of the Lamb.

Worship will fill every time and space in the end, even very soon,

as every knee bows and every tongue confesses that Christ is truly

the King of Kings and Lord of Lords, Messiah, Master, Ruler of all.

I'll start now.

My Was joins every Was all the way back to the first breath drawn by Adam.

(Does praise ever die? Does it not go on and on and on, perfuming the Throne Room forever?)

My Is joins all who now cry, "Holy, holy, holy is the Lord God Almighty, Who was, Who is,

Who is to come!," through every place in heaven and earth.

My Is-To-Come anticipates walking in His presence,

dwelling in His temple,

fully beholding His beauty,

and moving in His power and authority forever.

Glory to glory.

Strength to strength.

Abiding in Him for timeless ages,

whether in flesh or in heaven.

> *"I am the Alpha and Omega, the Beginning and the End," says the Lord, "who is and who was and who is to come, the Almighty." Revelation 1:8*

He Comes to *Battle*

I don't send only My Name and the voice and power
of My Blood to your defense,

I come to battle.

Myself.

My Presence.

*My feet standing on your ground, taking it back, making
it holy, staking My Name over it.*

Do you not sense Me near?

Have I not manifested My Spirit within you?

Then *know,* Child, to Whom the battle belongs.

Me.

The Holy One, Sanctifier, Redeemer, Deliverer, Healer,
Ancient of Days, Lord Sabaoth,

Mighty-to-Save, Resurrected One,

with resurrection power in hand.

You can't yet see it, I know.

But you can trust Me.

I alone know the time and way.

I treasure your delight.

I weep with you.

And I, the One who has named you My precious
Beloved, am moving.

It will be done.

It has begun.

Look up, stand tall, watch, expect.

Satan cannot stay where I stand.

> *"...do not be afraid nor dismayed by this
> great multitude,
> for the battle is not yours, but God's." 2
> Chronicles 20:15b*

Glory

Glory lives inside you.
Christ in you—Christ, the Beautiful One, Magnificent
Son, templing in you—
Oh, the hope of Glory!
Glory that fills and spills out no matter where you are,
mountain or valley.
Glory that leaps up and rejoices,
no matter what the circumstance.
Glory perfectly fitted to your life and purpose.
Light. Gifts. Calling. Beauty of the Lord.
Evil schemes have tried to hinder…but let's do it anyway.
Stand firm, strong, full of abundant life,
and watch what Satan meant for evil be turned
and reversed into great good.

*To them God willed to make known what
are the riches of the glory
of this mystery among the Gentiles:
which is Christ in you,
the hope of glory. Colossians 1:27*

What Do You *Ask For?*

What is it you ask for, Child?

Oh, my King, my faithful Love, my tender Father,
I ask for *You.*

You, as the Spirit, working in the deepest of the deep.

You, as Redeemer, pouring Blood over all that requires
its cleansing.

You, as Restorer of all the thief has stolen.

You, as the One who fills our inner man,

and loves, convicts, speaks, heals, bears fruit, illumines, guides, delights.

You, as the Father, Who is all wise.

You, as the Son, Who bought our souls.

You, as the Spirit, Who dares dwell in simple vessels.

You, mighty King, as the armor, the defense, the
worker of miracles,

the One and Only before Whom nothing is impossible,

the One before Whom all of heaven bows and sings,

crying out in deepest praise to the magnificent Most High.

You, having Your way,
doing all You planned for this little soul.

*Well then, Child, **watch Me**.*
You can so completely trust Me.

> *"Ask, and you will receive, that your joy may be full." John 16:24b*

> *"...and you are complete in Him...".*
> *Colossians 2:10*

I Stepped In

I have spoken Truth to you, Child.

You can count on it, trust it, believe it.

I know your emotions.

I know they are deep and tender,

and I know they have been so wounded.

The wound is not fatal.

It will destroy nothing,

but will be a spiritual marker that,

in the day of intense battle,

the frontline warfare,

the moment the enemy planned to plunge your heart with

everything he thought would destroy you—

I stepped in.

Said enough. Exposed the plots. Called your name.

In the day of destruction and torment, of despair and darkness,

I came.

I am here.

I did not for a moment leave your side,

but only allowed what could be used as a grand set-up
for glory.

For praise.

For rejoicing that is deeper because of the battle.

Joy is good on pleasant days,

but how much richer it is when it comes on the heels
of a mighty victory!

You will know that joy, Child.

So deep, so pure,

so abundant and overflowing.

Go ahead and walk in it.

You are the delight of My heart.

> *"But as for you, you meant evil against me;*
> *but God meant it for good, in order to*
> *bring it about as it is this day,*
> *to save many people alive." Genesis 50:20*

The Tallit

(prayer shawl)

My heart comes under the Tallit, my King.
Tabernacle with me here.
Meet with me fresh and unveil the deep,
the healing, the beauty, the power,
the shelter, the purest love.
There is no other place.
There is no one but You.
I pour out my heart—come, pour out Your Spirit.
Soak every nook and cranny of my very core
till all is bathed in Truth
and soaked in Spirit.
Oh, Father, I so love You.
I come as Your child under Your strong arm,
and I rest my soul.
Send Your Word, and heal me.

My heart moves at your words, My Child.
I will move yours at Mine.
I will show you My beauty.
I will do all I have said.

> "But to you who fear My name the Sun of
> Righteousness shall arise
> with healing in His wings..." Malachi 4:2

Prayer for My Children

Because I am in covenant with You, Most High God,
and because of the power of the Name and Blood of
Jesus Christ,
Son of God and Son of Man, Messiah, Deliverer,
Master, King of Kings soon coming,
I enter boldly to the Secret Place,
and ask for my children.
Image bearers of You.
Carriers of my blood, redeemed by Yours.
Go into the deep, Holy Spirit.
Expose and uproot lies long believed,
and let Truth take root and grow.
Send Your Word to crash walls, soothe spirits and
fully heal.
Fully heal.
Spirit, Soul and Body, all reflecting divine grace.
Run to them, Jesus.
Grab hold of their hearts and direct their directions.
Let nothing blanket their truest selves—

the truth of who they were crafted to be,
the beautiful essence deposited by You.
Clear, cleanse, heal, anoint and send forth unhindered.
Forward feet set to run the race,
enveloped in love and full of great, inexpressible joy.
Such joy is such strength!
Every tiny step, every huge leap,
led only by You, Lord.
So be it, Lord.
In Jesus' name.

> *Let us therefore come boldly to the
> throne of grace,
> that we may find grace to help in time of
> need. Hebrews 4:16*

> *I have no greater joy than to hear that my
> children walk in truth. 3 John 1:4*

There Is a Plan

There is a plan, My Love.
I am not random
and never surprised.
You are written on My palm,
and your days are purposed with great joy.
Don't allow pain to open Despair's door.
You are safe.
I am all that I am—
Healer, Restorer, Builder, Redeemer,
Shepherd, Father, Provider,
Lover of all your soul.
Don't be afraid, Love.
I am, and I am good.
I am faithful to My Word.
And *it shall be.*

"For I know the thoughts that I think
toward you," says the Lord,
"thoughts of peace and not of evil,
to give you a future and a hope."
Jeremiah 29:11

Say So

Oh, Child.

You are redeemed—*say so.*

You are seated with Me in heavenly places—*rest in that knowledge.*

You are filled with My Spirit—*trust Me.*

I am faithful.

My promises are "yes" and "amen" in Christ.

It is unfolding in beauty, My Love.

Do not fear.

I have not forgotten one word.

> *Let the redeemed of the Lord say so....*
> *Psalm 107:2*

Holy Ground

I am holy ground, Child.
On this ground all falls into place,
all comes into alignment,
all stands in what it really is.
I know you.
I know who you are—
the real, precious you.
It remains intact, though so battered,
and I will cause it to arise, to shine, to become,
to bear light to so much darkness.
My opinion only, dear Child, counts.
And I so, so love you.
I am, Child,
and in Me you really are.

> *Arise, shine; for your light has come!*
> *And the glory of the Lord is risen upon*
> *you. Isaiah 60:1*

He Sees

I am with you, Child.
I see those things that cut deep and wound much.
I see the open heart.
I see where the enemy has taken much ground.
You are safe, My Love.
No fear here.
For I also see Blood and Spirit pouring out on your behalf,
and I see victory that is Mine alone to give.
I give it to you, Love.
It is yours.
You have asked,
you have surrendered,
and I have seen.
The strength your eyes will see, Love,
is more than your mind can imagine.

For the eyes of the Lord run to and fro throughout the whole earth, to show Himself strong
on behalf of those whose heart is loyal to Him. 2 Chronicles 16:9a

I Feel

Lord, I feel...
It doesn't matter what you feel, Child,
*it matters **who I am** and what I have said—*
that word of Truth spoken on your behalf.
Feelings lie,
and the enemy takes advantage of them.
I am for you.
That is enough.
Love Me with heart, mind, *soul,* and strength.
Mind, will and emotions that are fixed on Me and worship Me
will be whole,
on guard, shielded
and greatly usable to build My Kingdom—
a high call and privilege.

Set your mind on things above, not on things on the earth. Colossians 3:2

You will keep him in perfect peace, whose mind is stayed on You, because he trusts in You. Isaiah 26:3

He Knows

I know, Child. I know.
You don't have to wonder if I am aware of
those re-occurring knife wounds.
Am I not Comforter and Counselor?
Do I not promise never to leave?
Are My plans not good?
Do not fear, Child,
though the enemy tries to stir up waves.
You are safe.
Never forsaken.
I am able, and I *know.*
My wing shelters you.
My promises ring loud and true
and are forever established in the heavens.
They *will* come to pass.
Rest your weary heart here.

"Be strong and of good courage, do not fear nor be afraid of them;
for the Lord your God, He is the one who goes with you.
He will not leave or forsake you."
Deuteronomy 31:6

Victory Is Sure

There is none like Me, Child.
Believe it in the core of all you are.
Yes, the enemy stirs waves of pain and discouragement,
but MY Word calms the storm.
It is finished—*and victory is sure.*
So, so sure.
Rejoice in Me, Child, and stand your ground.
Greater am I—nothing escapes My eyes—
and all I have spoken I will so surely do.
Great is My faithfulness and lavish My mercy.
Sweet, bruised reed, I am here.
I will act.
Do not fear.

> *Through the Lord's mercies we are*
> *not consumed,*
> *because His compassions fail not.*
> *They are new every morning;*
> *great is Your faithfulness.*
> *Lamentations 3:22-23*

Prayer

There is a continual, ever-lived-in *lifestyle* of prayer,
but there is also the sweet, sweet time of tucked away,
quiet, closeted in with the King prayer.
Hearts poured out to Father prayer.
Words can't wrap around the beauty, the mystery,
the soul calming, mountain moving power
that spills out there.
Such fullness.
Matchless grace swelling up and pouring out.
Abundant life begins here.
Fiery answers originate here.
Angels are commanded from words uttered here.
What begins in still, small whispers ends in earth-shaking,
divine intervention.
Impossibilities unfold into reality here.
Humble, aching hearts are fully healed here.
No wonder the enemy tries to drive us away from the
sacred chamber.
Come to Me, sweet, weary one,

and I'll give your heart rest.

> *The effective, fervent prayer of a righteous man avails much. James 5:16*

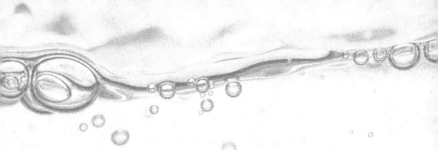

It Came To Pass

And it came to pass...

that My faithfulness poured into your very present reality,

and all My words to you became a place you no longer dream of or hope for,

but *walk in*.

A place of waiting's reward,

where your mustard seed well planted becomes a mighty tree,

where many find rest, shade and sustaining fruit.

I do not promise and fail to perform.

I do not express love words and fail to accompany them with action.

You have clung to My faithfulness, dear Child *(I love you so!)*,

and it was not in vain.

Never in vain.

Much awaits, My Love.

Look, the Door is open!

Go through the gates with praise,
enter the Promise with thanksgiving.

> *Enter into His gates with thanksgiving,*
> *and into His courts with praise.*
> *Be thankful to Him, and bless His name.*
> *Psalm 100:4*

His Voice

Voice as the sound of many waters,
Voice that creates from nothing,
    that splits rocks and tombs and utter darkness,
Voice whose words go forth in matchless power
    and everlasting effectiveness,
    whose commands and promises are "yes" and "Amen"
in Christ Jesus,
    and whose every jot and tittle come to fulfillment,
    into full blown, lived out and danced in reality…
please, Word of the Most High,
Voice of the One True God,
matchless, mighty Holy Spirit,
please speak here.
Burst through cords and chains and shackles and
strongholds
    and generations of darkness,
    and please,
    speak the *indeed freedom of Christ.*
Here.

Today.

In this.

> *And I heard a voice from heaven, like the*
> *voice of many waters,*
> *and like the voice of loud thunder...*
> *Revelation 14:2*
>
> *"My sheep hear My voice, and I know*
> *them, and they follow Me." John 10:27*

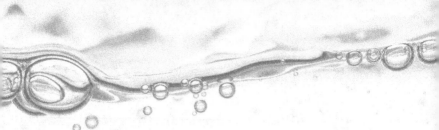

Water on the Stones

I am rushing water, Child,
pouring into your nooks and crannies
and never-reached heart crevices.
I have always seen them.
Your depths are fixed in My vision.
I have been moving deeper and deeper within,
until you were ready for My full outpouring.
Full, rushing, cleansing,
healing *life* poured over all—
even what you so long held back.
My water smooths stones,
and those stones will be hurled against your Goliath
in great victory!
Stony hearts no more,
but stones of victory.
Stones of memorial.
Jewel stones.
Ephod stones.
Oh, it's so, so good, Child!

"I will give you a new heart and put a new
spirit within you;
I will take the heart of stone out of
your flesh and
give you a heart of flesh." Ezekiel 36:26

I Am With You

I am with you, Child.

In the waves and torments and terrors,

in the arrows that fly and thoughts that capture—

still I am with you.

I know your frame, My Love;

I remember the weakness of flesh.

So I pour *fresh* on you, Love.

Fresh vision. Fresh hope. Fresh anointing.

Fresh fire, burning within.

I fan that flame, sweet, dear, Love;

I give it energy and far-reaching light.

Relax into Me.

Don't look at your own realm, intellect, ability…

Solely focus on My Word and My Spirit,

and all will fall into place.

I am the Author.

I am the Perfecter,

and I will absolutely be the Finisher.

For He knows our frame;
He remembers that we are dust.
Psalm 103:14

...looking unto Jesus,
the author and finisher of our faith....
Hebrews 12:2a

It Shall Be

Wrapped in Your faithfulness, what do I have to fear?
How can lack and despair consume,
when the King has spoken love?
Covenant cloaks—the rich, glorious, matchless
inheritance—
and anointing's power breaks yokes.
The word of my Father is settled secure and brightly
in the heavens,
and what word of mere flesh can overturn what the
King has declared?
It will be.
It shall be done.
It is even now coming to pass,
being formed in Father's heart of love
and carried forth into the realm of men.
The holy spoken, declared, formed in the Throne
Room of God
and delivered by Spirit and Truth into the heart of *you*,
beloved, precious One.

Nothing can withstand His Word.

No darkness can refuse to flee.

No weapon can find ground to prosper.

No evil can overrule.

Faithful and True has decreed the thing.

Bow, worship, seek,

and you shall absolutely find the doors of promise and prophecy

flung wide before you.

> *Forever, O Lord, Your word is settled in heaven.*
> *Your faithfulness endures to all generations. Psalm 119:89-90*
>
> *"...the word of our God stands forever."*
> *Isaiah 40:8*

That Power

That power shakes within you—
power that causes boulders to tremble,
mountains to roll back,
chains to melt to dust.
Power that welled up within crucified Christ
and put Him on His mighty feet.
Power that allowed a dark season in order to reveal
its depths and conquering strength,
so that it can now be funneled from the Throne
directly into you.
No power can match it.
No enemy can defeat it.
It reigns in you,
it fills and floods and fully equips you.
And before that power, Love, what can stand in
opposition?
What can scream, "Impossible!"
when that same force operates within your
earthen vessel?

Don't fear, Love.
Believe,
and let Me work Resurrection in you.

> *...that you may know...what is the*
> *exceeding greatness of His power*
> *toward us who believe, according to the*
> *working of His mighty power*
> *which He worked in Christ when He*
> *raised Him from the dead and*
> *seated Him at His right hand in the*
> *heavenly places. Ephesians 1:19-20*

Fuel

No other fuel for the fire within—
just Him—
always Him…
was Him, is Him, all to come is Him.
Any other flame will quickly extinguish
before enemy's hot breath of lies.
Only Truth's fire will last forever—
never leaving, never forsaking,
never dimming…

> *But the Word of the Lord endures for-
> ever. 1 Peter 1:25*
>
> *"Is not My Word like a fire?" says the Lord,
> "And like a hammer that breaks the rock
> in pieces?" Jeremiah 23:29*

A Plan

I have a plan.

Just because you don't yet see it does not ever mean it isn't in place,

already decreed and established in the heavens.

You adore My Word;

My Word will direct you.

It is not dependent on man.

Do not fear, Love.

It will be.

He cares for His household *so well,*

does He not?

Is there lack with Him?

Does He not over-pay His servants,

and lavish His children with every good and perfect gift?

Your worries are over small things, Child.

I am not blind or unjust.

I do not give My Word and refuse to fulfill it.

Abraham was *put to sleep* as I cut covenant.
I have this.
You do not need to strive or fear.
Your children are provided for and blessed.
I have heard your Mother heart.
It is done.

> *"For I know the thoughts that I think toward you," says the Lord,*
> *"thoughts of peace and not of evil, to give you a future and a hope." Jeremiah 29:11*

One More

One more day to choose faith over fear.
One more day to choose to move forward.
One more day to look at the blessings—
to search them out and give praise for them,
and one more day to scatter their abundance.
One more day to stand on earthly soil
and pray the glory of His Kingdom come,
to this place,
in these things.
One more day to offer all to the soon-coming King
for His delight and use.

I will trust You in this day, Lord.
This day I will once again ask for Your Spirit
of wisdom,
of resurrection power,
of knowledge of Christ.
I will ask again for eyes to see,
ears to hear,

and feet to move forward.
For Your beautiful glory.

> *This is the day the Lord has made; we will*
> *rejoice and be glad in it. Psalm 118:24*

> *Whenever I am afraid, I will trust in You.*
> *In God (I will praise His Word),*
> *in God I have put my trust; I will not fear.*
> *Psalm 56:3-4*

Centered

I come back to the Foundation, the Rock,
the solid, sure, steady ground of Christ,
of Love,
and I center myself there.
I release to the Righteous Judge all that has wounded
and offended,
and command it to leave my presence.
I ask to be refilled, to overflow, with His goodness,
His wisdom,
His heart and mind.
Out of this core, this center,
all of life will be affected.
"Guard your heart, for out of it flow the issues of life."
Keep the core centered,
anchored in that place where heart can calm,
slow down,
go into a peaceful, restful place,
regardless of circumstances.
A place for anxieties to melt away, giving place to *hope*—

the thing that looks forward with expectation
to see God move.

Lift me up out of the destructive flow of flesh
thoughts, Lord Jesus.
Those streams of thought that rush right into
destruction,
straight into bitterness,
headlong into heartache and unholy decisions and
reactions.
Cover me, Holy Spirit.
Fix my heart fully on Christ, on His beauty, His
wonder, His healing balm,
His majestic glory and unfathomably deep love.
Anchor me there in a new stream,
a living River, a pure and satisfying wellspring.
Holy Spirit and Truth of God, raise Your
mighty Sword and
crush through walls flesh has built and pain
has cemented,
and let every trace of pent-up poison be released
and cast far from my being and realm of influence.
In Jesus' Name and because of His Blood—
so be it.

*"Therefore whoever hears these sayings
of Mine, and does them,
I will liken him to a wise man who built
his house on the rock." Matthew 7:24*

*Keep your heart with all diligence, for out
of it spring the issues of life. Prov.4:23*

I Am the Lord

I am the Lord,
the Lord strong and mighty,
mighty to save.
Have I said, and will I not do?
Have I declared, and will I not perform?
Have I sent My Word to fall to the ground?
Oh, sweet Child,
I am moving in the unseen.
I am arranging, designing,
bringing forth wonders from on high
into your realm.
Rejoice, Love.
I have not forgotten one word whispered to you,
even though you possibly have.
Do not fear.
You will not miss My outpouring.
Come, Love.
Follow Me.

Who is this King of Glory? The Lord strong and mighty,
the Lord mighty in battle! Lift up your heads, O you gates!
Lift up, you everlasting doors!
And the King of Glory shall come in.
Who is this King of Glory?
The Lord of hosts, He is the King of Glory. Psalm 24:8-10

Be Wise

Do not be unwise, but wise in these days.
They are dark, but, behold, I am doing a new thing,
bringing forth a new level of anointing.
For even as darkness is over the people and is released
with great fury upon earth,
yet greater and deeper still is the pouring forth of Truth,
by My Spirit,
that is about to take place.
It will not come from the expected places,
from the highest, visible, decreed places.
It will come from hearts bent low
that seek Me.
Only Me.
Not riches, fame or recognition.

Rejoice, Love! Again I say, rejoice!
What is built on My foundation,
on the True and only Rock,
who is Jesus Christ, the Son of the Living God,

shall forever stand.

I order, I build, I join together, I establish.

Stone upon stone, small upon small,

cemented to true and firm Foundation,

whose walls the wolf cannot blow down,

and whose heartbeat and pulse will be My very breath.

> *If any of you lacks wisdom, let him ask*
> *of God, who gives to all liberally*
> *and without reproach, and it will be*
> *given to him. James 1:5*

> *For behold, the darkness shall cover the*
> *earth, and deep darkness the people;*
> *but the Lord will arise over you, and His*
> *glory will be seen upon you. Isaiah 60:2*

The Breath

The Breath that always was,
that pulses in power today,
that stretches out beyond forever...
the Breath that condensed into Babe
and for a time breathed among men,
that seemed silenced for three days,
but then filled holy lungs and exhaled
the greatest Victory...
the Breath scripted in red and
formed into Sword that will never fail,
be found untrue,
or fall to the ground...
that forever Breath breathes new into you.
That mighty Breath swells within
and raises you also from death.
Breath fills heart and forms life words on tongue,
and what is spoken is not mere man words,

but heaven's power funneled into lives of men.
Breathe deep, Child.
It is good.

> *And when He had said this, He breathed*
> *on them, and said to them,*
> *"Receive the Holy Spirit." John 20:22*

At His Feet

I'm so thankful to be able to come to His Feet,
the beautiful Feet that bear Salvation's scars,
that walked the earth and know my pain,
that bore Calvary's weight and on that mountain
brought the Gospel of Peace.
I fall before them,
I pour the tears and perfume of my heart on them,
I kiss them and wipe them with my hair.
I am welcomed with sweet tenderness;
my heart tears are gladly received.
Rejection pours on those Feet,
and its sting is dissolved.
Disappointment and disillusionment spill out,
and are replaced with calm.
Urgency of the times brings urgent pleas…
Oh, the Feet.
Bless You, my King.

Run, weary one!
You have come to My feet, and I have strengthened yours.

> ...and she began to wash His feet with
> her tears,
> and wiped them with the hair of her head,
> and she kissed His feet and anointed
> them with the fragrant oil. Luke 7:38

You

You take what is emptied out
and pour a refilling I knew not existed.
You settle anxiety's waves
and speak in that still, small whisper.
You cup my face as it spills its waters,
then lovingly bandage my war-torn wounds—
and you tell me to rise.
To shine.
New, equipped, enabled to stand.
You tend to my feet, as I have come to Yours,
and You set me in position,
in calling, in anointing,
filled with fresh strength.
You are so good.
Bless Your Name, Jesus the Christ,
Son of God and Son of Man,
Everlasting, Wonderful,

Counselor, Prince of Peace,
Lord of Lords,
King of all Kings.

> *For the Lord is good; His mercy is*
> *everlasting,*
> *and His truth endures to all generations.*
> *Psalm 100:5*

This Day

This is the day the Lord has made;
I will rejoice and be glad in it.
This day—now—this very present time frame
is filled with His very present help,
and Grace flows from the Throne
directly into the time of man.
This day has been given life and breath.
This day has the blessed assurance of the King's presence
in Spirit and Truth.
This day is planned for and purposed in Father's heart
to be well used,
to bring pieces of His great Mission into place.
This day is destiny.
So rejoice!
Let a shout ring loud in your soul!
For *this day,*
no matter the pain of past or uncertainty of future,
will surely serve to bridge the two

into a thing of great beauty and much splendor.
This day is the Lord's,
and He has graciously gifted it to you.
Run well.
Be glad, for it is a new day!
You have a new heart—a new spirit is planted deep
within you—
and all Father said
He will do.
Even today.

> *This is the day the Lord has made; we will
> rejoice and be glad in it. Psalm 118:24*

See

See yourself whole, My Child.
Body, soul, spirit made well in My strength.
My Blood spilled for *all* of you.
Its power pours out
and flows into your *entire* being.
It is not given just for "someday" heaven,
for a time when tent folds
and spirit soars to My Throne Room,
but for a very present help.
As a man thinks, *so is he.*
Thoughts sink down into your being
and work themselves into your reality.
Again, Love,
see yourself whole.

> *For as he thinks in his heart, so is he.*
> *Proverbs 23:7*

My Words

My Words,
oh, My Words to you, Child,
are full and rich,
they are healing and power,
they are Truth and life,
and they will forever change you.
They will seep into deepest crevices of darkest places
and will *blaze glory*.
They will envelope and destroy long-held deceptions,
and will let freedom ring.
They will wash over heart, soul, mind and strength,
and will utterly and completely transform.
They are a gift to you—
precious, priceless, everlasting.
Open wide your mouth,
and I will fill to overflow.

"I am the Lord your God, who brought
you out of the land of Egypt.
Open your mouth wide, and I will fill it."
Psalm 81:10

"...I have treasured the words of His
mouth more than my necessary food."
Job 23:12b

Fulfilled

Oh, the beauty of every jot and tittle fulfilled,
every Word breathed by the Most High
quickened and brought to life,
every promise burned in spirit
coming to pass in present, living, active reality.
Soul-stirring, faith-building,
amazing answers to heart cries—
the overwhelming intervention of the Lord in a life,
the power of the Sword wielded
and deep victory tasted.
Oh, the Word of our God becomes
the word of our testimony
that, by the Blood of Jesus,
makes us more than conquerors.

*"If you abide in Me, and My Words
abide in you,
you will ask what you desire, and it shall
be done for you." John 15:7*

*"Ask, and it will be given to you; seek,
and you will find;
knock, and it will be opened to you."
Matthew 7:7*

His Love

*I love **you**, Child—*
not just My plans for you.
Yes, I want to unfold the divine in your life,
but first ***I love.***
I don't see you just as someone to use,
but as My dearest,
whom I *love to be with,*
whom I enjoy,
one who is a delight to walk with and speak to.
I don't just employ you—
I adore you.
I want your friendship,
not just your gifts.

> "No longer do I call you servants, for a
> servant does not know what his master
> is doing; but I have called you friends,
> for all things that I heard from My Father
> I have made known to you." John 15:15

Water of Word

Oh, His Words are almost too holy and beautiful to bear.

Such power breathed into profane vessels,

such blast of cleansing and life,

of strength and joy.

The water of the Word—*liquid life on written page*—

pouring into brittle desert.

Where it goes, *abundant life springs up.*

Wash over me, holy Water,

and cleanse the Self places,

the Bitter places,

the Shut-Down places,

the Sorrow places.

I want to operate fully in Resurrection Power,

in grace and Truth,

in Love and faith.

Have Your way, Word of God.

You are the Way.

"...everything will live wherever the river goes." *Ezekiel 47:9b*

...that He might sanctify and cleanse her with
the washing of water by the word... *Ephesians 5:26*

Shepherd

Shepherd leads you to healing streams of Living Water
that meets the deepest, driest places
with renewing life.
He gives you pasture, sanctuary,
rest for your soul.
He feeds you from His hand,
and soothes you with
His Words of comfort and delight.
He restores all that was stolen or lost
with double portion.
You can trust Him.

> *The Lord is my shepherd; I shall not want.*
> *He makes me to lie down in*
> *green pastures;*
> *He leads me beside the still waters.*
> *He restores my soul;*
> *He leads me in paths of righteousness*
> *for His name's sake. Psalm 23:1-3*

Restore

Restore our souls, Lord,

to who we are in Your pure eyes

before the failure,

the deepest of wounds, the weakness,

the life pain.

Cleanse us fully;

wash our feet from the caked mud of flesh,

and set us upright, anchored

in the Vision only Your Spirit can give.

Let us go fully and freely into the embracing of call,

the sharing of every good and perfect gift,

the releasing of the Flow with which

You have flooded our souls.

Blood was given so we can become who we really are...

and be restored as pure before God.

Thank You, dear King.

*Therefore, if anyone is in Christ, he is a
new creation;
old things have passed away; behold, all
things have
become new. 2 Corinthians 5:17*

He restores my soul. Psalm 23:3

Graced

I have graced you, Child.
It floods and fills and spills out
into all you are.
Not ever are you defined by man's terms
or by their flesh-based words,
but you are forever
who I declare you to be.
You have known bitter words,
but they have not found a place to grow.
You have bent low under crushing rejections
but have not fallen,
for My own hand has defended you
and lifted you up to newness
and passion.
You are more than a conqueror,
more than victorious,
more than you know.
I do not lie,

nor do I tease.
I will do all I have said.
It is well, Child.
It is well.

> *Yet in all these things we are more than
> conquerors
> through Him who loved us. Romans 8:37*

Fire

My Word is a lamp for your feet—
a burning fire before you.
Fire of God that consumes and blinds enemy,
that fans flame of wonder
and awe,
that leaps within and stirs your very core.
Holy fire that blazes the trail,
that burns in bush,
that calls you out of darkness
into marvelous light.
Fire that makes a place for you.
Enter in.
It's holy ground.

*Your Word is a lamp to my feet and a
light to my path. Psalm 119:105*

*But His Word was in my heart like a
burning fire shut up in my bones;
I was weary of holding it back, and I
could not. Jeremiah 20:9*

Emotions

Don't apologize for emotions, My Love.
I gave them to you as a gift,
as a tender stream,
as an outflow of Myself.
I don't want your emotions *numbed*—
I want them *healed,*
made whole,
with a heart of flesh rather than stone.

Let right, holy,
Throne-Room-derived emotions
fill me, Lord.
Let them add to Your glory and lead
in compassion.
Let them not be ruled by flesh
or darkness,
and let them never steer my life into
self-focus.
Jesus wept—

with compassion.
Let all my outpouring be the same.

I am stronger than your emotions,
deeper than their deepest vein,
longer, wider, higher
than their most despairing cry.
You are surrounded.
You are safe.
Pain can never outlast My love.
I declared, "It is finished,"
so you can absolutely rest your heart on the
knowledge that,
in My finished work,
there is an absolute end to the things that seek to torment
and cripple your heart.
I am leading you that you may lead.
It is good.

Jesus wept. John 11:35

Put my tears into Your bottle; are they
not in Your book? Psalm 56:8b

A New Day

I am with you in the darkness and stillness of night, Child.

I cloak you as you rest at My feet.

Night has an end, Love!

Look up—

it's the dawn of a new day!

See, I did not forget My promises to you,

though they seemed to stretch long.

My timing is beautiful and perfect,

far above what you could have imagined.

See, it is so good!

So powerful and effective.

Healing is sweet, Love.

And so sweet to share.

Arise, shine; for your light has come!
And the glory of the Lord is risen upon
you. Isaiah 60:1

"But to you who fear My Name the Sun
of Righteousness shall arise
with healing in His wings..." Malachi 4:2

Resist and *Rebuild*

Do you see patterns of darkness, Child?
Can you identify enemy channels
that have long tormented?
Name them before Me.
Rejoice in My power over them!
Submit to Me.
Come under My wing of strength and grace,
and *resist those things by faith.*
They *must* flee,
and the foul spirits that carry them
must go
at the sound of My Name and
the eternal covering of My Blood.
Hearts swept clean,
then never left empty and dry,
but *filled, refreshed, soaked,*
saturated to overflow with the living, breathing,
speaking, fully operating

Spirit of the Living God.
And the Rebuilding begins.

> *Therefore submit to God. Resist the devil and he will flee from you. James 4:7*

> *"You are of God, little children, and have overcome them, because He who is in you is greater than he who is in the world." 1 John 4:4*

> *And they shall rebuild the old ruins, they raise up the former desolations,*
> *and they shall repair the ruined cities, the desolations of many generations."*
> *Isaiah 61:4*

Mercy Seeps

There's a steady stream, Child,
dripping in the cracks and caverns
and mingling with your tears.
Mercy seeps into the deepest,
most impassable wedges
and speaks piercingly,
directly to your soul.

I did not cause this wound.
My face never turned away.
But, dear, sweet, Child,
use it I will.
Did Joseph not see years stretch long in captivity?
But was it not being woven into a place of positioning
that would call into darkness and desperation
and *speak life*, fullness, health,
restoration of things he never dreamed of?
He did, My Love.
And so shall you.

Let go of discouragement.
Bleed before Me,
for I can heal.
I can do what no man can.
You are safe, Child.
Rest here.
Don't give it space in your mind or heart.
Focus on Me.

> *But You, O Lord, are a God full of com-*
> *passion, and gracious, long suffering and*
> *abundant in mercy and truth.*
> *Psalm 86:15*

I Know

I know where you are, Child.
It is not My love or My plans
that have been misplaced.
It is not your worth or destiny
that are forgotten or overlooked.
Do I not see the depth and core?
Do My eyes not drink in Beginning and End?
Can you, who only grasp a mere slice of time,
determine the due season
and greatest outcome?
Oh, dear Child.
Did Joseph not linger long in that place of question?
Did betrayal not have to be worked out of his heart
and Destiny worked in?
Training ground is NOT forsaken ground.
Birthing in pain and darkness
does not mean Light and joy are not soon to come.
You are seen, My Love.

I Know

You are watched with great delight.
Grace surrounds in ways you cannot yet see,
and Glory will soon fill your skies!

> *O Lord, You have searched me and known me. You know my sitting down and my rising up; you understand my thought afar off. You comprehend my path and my lying down, and are acquainted with all my ways. Psalm 139:1-3*
>
> *And there is no creature hidden from His sight... Hebrews 4:13a*

More

The King is in this place.
Holy is the ground on which you stand.
Mighty is the strength beneath you.

It is good, Child.
I am here.
I am doing more than you asked,
more than you knew to imagine.
More, Child.
There is so much more.
Do not grieve seasons past,
but rejoice in glorious seasons
to come!
I will turn your face to joy, My Love.

Though you have suffered long,
you have faithfully remained
in My tender embrace,

and I will openly reward you.
It is good, Love.

> *Now to Him who is able to do exceed-*
> *ingly abundantly above all that we ask or*
> *think, according to the power that works*
> *in us, to Him be glory in the church by*
> *Christ Jesus to all generations, forever*
> *and ever. Amen. Ephesians 3:20-21*

Bring Forth

In this new season, my King,
bring forth the Ancient of Days.
In this day of promise,
bring forth full redemption.
Let eyes be opened
and ears be unstopped;
let hearts drink in and
rejoice fully in the Word walked out.
Re-order, renew, transform.
In this time,
let what is Timeless define us.
Strengthen us in the inner core,
solid as a mighty oak by living waters.
Settle us in the innermost places, Lord,
so our hearts are set upon the Rock,
immovable.
So much has blasted,

but You have held.
Bless Your Name, my King.

> *For this reason I bow my knees*
> *to the Father of our Lord Jesus*
> *Christ, from whom*
> *the whole family in heaven and*
> *earth is named, that He would grant*
> *you, according*
> *to the riches of His glory, to be strength-*
> *ened with might through His Spirit in the*
> *inner man... Ephesians 3:14-16*

Love

When love surrounds and envelopes,
encouraging and bringing safety of heart,
there soul flourishes, prospers,
tastes victory and success.
There is but one Love able
to fill every heart crevice;
only one Love
that so perfectly casts out fear.
Man does not possess it.
Man can, and is purposed to,
funnel its flow into a dark and lonely world,
but its Source is solitary.
Love in man is but a fruit,
a product of, the love of God.
It is implanted by Holy Spirit
and nurtured in Truth.
It surrounds and fills,
envelopes and protects,

casts out fear and anxiety...
and in it,
your heart can truly prosper.

> *...that you, being rooted and grounded in love, may be able to comprehend with all the saints what is the width and length and depth and height—to know the love of Christ which passes knowledge; that you may be filled with all the fullness of God. Ephesians 3:17-19*

> *There is no fear in love; but perfect love casts out fear... 1 John 4:18*

Command

Now the Day

I command my body, soul and spirit to come in line with the Word of God,

the Word made flesh,

the Word of life that fills, cleanses, heals.

Body—you are templed by the Spirit of the Most High God, and you are to be strong, free, functioning in health to carry the implanted Word.
Be whole, because of Jesus' sacrifice.

I submit this temple to Your keeping and dwelling, my King. I submit to habits of health, and I submit every cell and system to Your hands. Form vitality and strength there, Lord, and bring divine healing,

so that the casing for my soul and spirit will operate fully, without hindrance. I resist the temptations for unholy uses and destructions. Forgive and heal and seal every place I have fallen.

I receive strength, in Jesus' name.

Soul—inner core, drink deeply and be satisfied. Let fountains of living water rush into you and flow out. Be renewed and transformed. Let the mind of Christ, the will of God, fill you.
Be made new, because of Jesus' sacrifice.

I submit my mind, will and emotions to You, Lord, to Your Truth, to the mind of marvelous Jesus Christ, Living Son of Living God. I resist negative, destructive thoughts. I resist living by emotions. I ask that my will be lined up with and sanctified by Truth. I resist lying spirits and demonic suggestions. I resist foul and familiar spirits, and all generational curses.
I receive wisdom, revelation, knowledge of Christ, and the blessing and favor of God, in Jesus' name.

Spirit—listen and watch for Holy Spirit's movement, voice, interventions. Be sensitive to Him, *and thoroughly enjoy His company!!!*
Be one with God in sweet fellowship, because of Jesus' sacrifice.

I am eternal, and I submit every eternal part of me to the Eternal God, the Ancient of Days, Who Was, Who Is, Who Is To Come and sees beginning to end. I submit the breath within me and ask for the mighty, rushing, filling Breath of God. Breath that always resuscitates into full, abundant life, to overflow, so that other hearts will see and long for Him alone. I worship and pray in Spirit and Truth.
I receive His outpouring, in Jesus' name.

I bow and submit my all to the Most High, to Christ Jesus, the Lord of Lords and King of Kings, and I thank You, dear Father, for Your love and goodness— *and for Jesus' sacrifice.*

I receive the Shalom of God in Jesus' name!

> *Therefore submit to God. Resist the devil and he will flee from you. Draw near to God*
> *and He will draw near to you. James 4:7-8*
> *Beloved, I pray that you may prosper in all things and be in health, just as your soul prospers. 3 John 1:2*

Stand Your Ground

Oh, what beautiful ground given to my feet,
portioned for my soul...
fertile and nourishing to my spirit,
strengthening the inner core
and blossoming to bless.
Holy ground—
for the Lord stands with me.
Cleansed, sparkling, blazing-but-not-burning ground,
pure and spotless,
yet Blood soaked.
Safe here are you,
though storms batter
and seek to cause you to flee in fear.
Spirit of the Living God has called you to this place,
and you will not retreat,
lose ground
or stand paralyzed.
You stand in strength,
covered and shielded by the Mightiest One,

treasured, rooted,
planned for, prospered.
Stand in this soaking love, My dear Child.

> For no other foundation can anyone
> lay than that which is laid, which is
> Jesus Christ.
> 1 Corinthians 3:11

> "Take the sandals off your feet, for the
> place where you stand is holy ground."
> Exodus 3:5

I Bow

I bow my head before You, dear Lord,
to represent my heart, my mind, my soul and
my strength
prostrate before Your wisdom, Your majesty,
Your wonders, Your beauty, Your glory,
Your matchless Love poured out
to even me.
Take it all as Your own,
for Your own use and pleasure.
Take it all in these days,
as You pour Spirit to overflow.
Take it all, my King,
as one You can refine, train, renew.
Let no weapon formed prosper here.
Let no ground be left unguarded.
Let none of me rise up to interfere
with all Your good plans.
I am Yours, my King.

*I gladly, joyfully, thankfully submit all to
Your mighty and faithful keeping.*

> *Therefore humble yourselves under the
> mighty hand of God, that He may exalt
> you in due time, casting all your care
> upon Him, for He cares for you. 1
> Peter 5:6-7*

The Prayers

Oh, Father,
gather the prayers of the ages,
the fragrant incense
before Your Throne—
that beautiful bowl
before You—
and add mine to the Beauty.
Then stir them, Lord,
and pour out Your Spirit
with depths of power
we have only dared
touch the fringe of.

> Now when He had taken the scroll, the
> four living creatures and the twenty-four
> elders fell down before the Lamb, each
> having a harp, and golden bowls full of
> incense, which are the prayers of the
> saints. Revelation 5:8

Shaping

Fires refine, Child.
Though they have lapped hard
and threatened loud,
have they yet destroyed you?
Oh no, My Love.
They, meant for great evil,
have been forced to submit to only
shaping you,
never *destroying* you.
You will never be overcome.
You are more than a conqueror,
for you are in Me,
and I AM in you,
and *I shall never, never, never*
be overcome.
Neither, then, shall you.
Rise up.
Believe now, My Love,

for beauties are unfolding—
fragrant, tender, fresh, deep, powerful,
healthy—
and they will not only delight you,
but will pour out delight
even to the nations.

> *"...to give them beauty for ashes..."*
> *Isaiah 61:3a*

My Portion

In this midst of *this*, Child,
I am your portion.
In those places where so much has been stolen,
I am your inheritance.
I am the I AM.
No lack or shortage for you, My Love.
I know how darkness has wounded
and threatened
and sought to destroy all confidence,
but I will turn it and use it to show that
I am,
and in Me,
you are.
I have conquered,
so that you can also.
I have done the Great,
so that you can too.
I have loved the unlovable,

so you can as well.
Don't fear, Child.
Shalom.
And in fullness of Shalom,
mighty things flow.
Supernatural touch, healing, boldness,
Word prospering.

> *O Lord, You are the portion of my inher-*
> *itance and my cup;*
> *You maintain my lot. Psalm 16:5*

So Beautiful

I come before the Lord,
and my heart aches and groans
and sways beneath the weight
of the glory of His Word.
More beautiful than my flesh can bear.
So take me, my King,
in Spirit and Truth,
and fill me afresh
with more than I can contain.
Show me the flowing-out place, Lord.
Divine appointments.
Tender mercies shared.
Souls made whole.
Let me lose myself in Your Beauty,
Lord Jesus.
Waves of pure Truth,
washing Deception's death grip
from my very being.

"But the hour is coming, and now is, when the true worshippers will worship the Father in Spirit and Truth; for the Father is seeking such to worship Him." John 4:23

Peace

Peace, Child.
I have spoken—
My Word stands.
That's where you stand strong and firm,
unmoved by waves of trial—
in My Rhema breathed out to you.
Breathe deep, Child.
Let it fill all your being.
Though the enemy would use circumstances
to plant doubt in you—
you know Me.
And I know you.
You know well that I am with you,
that I am working out divine plans
and holy arrangements,
and that the enemy will not cause you to fall.
Stand in Me,
in the power of My might.

You are safe.
You are shielded by Blood impenetrable.
You are hidden in My Name.
It will be, Child, My sweet Love.
All I have spoken
is soon coming.

> And so we have the prophetic word con-
> firmed, which you do well to heed as
> a light that shines in a dark place, until
> the day dawns and the morning star
> rises in your hearts... 2 Peter 1:19

Fresh Mercy

Fresh mercy poured out in rushing, cleansing,
healing stream to my heart today—
calming the rush of life
and settling the depths and core.
Mercy to reorder, renew, and
transform this scattered, selfish mind.
Mercy to soothe, restore, and
redeem this aching soul.
Mercy held open,
inviting me to
cast my cares on Him.
So I do it, my King.
They are given fully to Your keeping…
let mercy heal my heart,
and use all for good.

*Through the Lord's mercies we are
not consumed, because His compas-
sions fail not.*
*They are new every morning; great is
Your faithfulness. Lamentations 3:22-23*

*Let us therefore come boldly to the throne
of grace, that we may obtain mercy
and find grace to help in time of need.
Hebrews 4:16*

Holy Script

Love poured out,
condensed into words of power meant to
fill up and ignite a heart—
to change a soul,
to bring into your life everything intended and
prepared for you by the
Most High God,
and to defeat enemies waiting at the gate,
bent on your destruction.

Hallelujah!
Thank You for Your mighty Word, my Father.
Holy Script sculpting holy hearts.

Open my eyes, that I may see wondrous
things from Your law. Psalm 119:18

Your testimonies are my delight and my
counselors. Psalm 119:24

Division

A spirit of division is at work, Child.
Dividing races, parties,
churches, families,
friendships...
Pray for Shalom.
Wholeness.
Ask, that you may receive.
People do not pray,
because they do not recognize the power
and the reality that comes with it.
Oh, *the power.*
Matchless, unceasing, limitless
power,
ready and full, available,
and offered by the Blood.
Watch, Love.
Watch what I do
when you pray.

The effective, fervent prayer of a righteous man avails much. James 5:16

Focus on Me

Come, Child.
focus on Me.
So much darkness swirls around you,
so much earth tries to drag your heart
into confusion and disruption.
I am here.
I am everything.
I am Beauty and Strength,
Healing and Delight.
Wonders plumb deep
and awe comes fresh
as you focus,
and look long,
at Me.
Eyes fixed,
not looking to another
to bring what only I can.
And I do.

I will.
I am ready, Love.
Watch.

> You will keep him in perfect peace,
> whose mind is stayed on You,
> because he trusts in You. Isaiah 26:3

> ...looking unto Jesus, the author and fin-
> isher of our faith... Hebrews 12:2

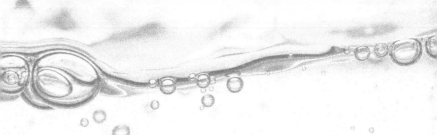

Holy Fire

Burning flame in earthly tent—
holy fire that consumes but does not destroy...

As Moses did before bush blazing with Glory,
take off your earth shoes.
Put on the Lord's—
the shoes of peace—
and bow low in His Presence.
This flame leaps not in shrub,
but in your *very soul—*
your own spirit,
your deepest core.

Oh, Spirit of God, I bow. Stir the depths and fan the
flame. Restore and pour forth all You have purposed for
this burning one in these days.

And that Fire will perfectly fuel my Race,
my Purpose,
my Destiny unfurling for Kingdom come.

No need for comparison or insecurity...
because there's a Race for *you, too,*
particular and purposeful,
with plenty of Fire to fuel.

Running together as
Carriers of Holy Flame—
encouraging, helping, doing good,
loving well—
true unity that releases blessing
and puts 10,000
to flight.

> *"Take your sandals off your feet, for the place where you stand is holy ground." Exodus 3:5*

> *...but His Word was in my heart like a burning fire shut up in my bones... Jeremiah 20:9*

> *But now indeed there are many members, yet one Body. 1 Corinthians 12:20*

Victory

I am Victory, My Love.
I cannot fail.
I cannot send out void Words.
I cannot refuse to bring into your reality
what I have declared to you.
See,
I do a new thing—
even now it comes into being.
I know.
I see your heart, My Love.
I am for you.
I AM.
And it all shall be.
You just trust your Abba,
your Beloved.

He sent His Word and healed them,
and delivered them from their destruc-
tions. Psalm 107:20

"These things I have spoken to you, that
in Me you may have peace.
In the world you will have tribulation;
but be of good cheer,
I have overcome the world." John 16:33

Don't Skip

Don't skip a step, My Love.
Don't rush ahead
before you have bowed low.
Receive there pure hands, clean heart,
washing, refreshing, renewing,
true inner-core cleansing
and transformation.
Then, Child,
oh then,
you are prepared with Truth,
energized by Spirit,
and humble in your knowledge
of My power.
I so love you.
I know it seems so strange that Blood
cleanses,
but in it dwells Life.

And I want you to have it
abundantly.

> "The thief does not come except to steal,
> and to kill, and to destroy.
> I have come that they may have life, and
> that they may have it
> more abundantly." John 10:10

Trust

Who am I, Love?
Am I not the Balm
for your bleeding soul,
the Speaker of Life
to your aching body,
the Restorer of all stolen
from your heart?
Am I not able
to take your overwhelming,
and overwhelm with Grace?
Trust My Love.
I know you cannot see how.
But those urgings and yearnings
deep within
will burst forth into an explosion
of Spirit outpoured.
I know the time, Love.
And I am never late.

Whenever I am afraid, I will trust in You.
Psalm 56:3

Prepare

Prepare your heart for Beauty today, Child.
Prepare it to receive today's portion of
unfolding Grace
and glorious Destiny.
Holy purpose wrapped in routine.
Let your heart expand to receive,
to let walls fall,
to let fear go
and believe
good and beautiful will come—
even to you.

> *So above all, guard the affections of your
> heart, for they affect all that you are.
> Pay attention to the welfare of your inner-
> most being, for from there flows the
> wellspring of life. Proverbs 4:3 (TPT)*

Come

Come to the Well early, My Love.
Come before the day begins,
before the mind starts to wander,
before earth's crustiness
and enemy flood have a chance
to overwhelm.
Let *My Voice* overwhelm—
the thundering sound as many waters
that falls as gentle rain
to your soul.
My Voice is life to you.
It is wisdom issued
from Throne to heart.
I have not failed you, My Love,
and *never* will I turn or abandon.
My plans remain.
My Words are established in heaven.
Come to the Well,

where it is well,
and *rest your soul.*

> *Now in the morning, having risen a long*
> *while before daylight,*
> *He went out and departed to a solitary*
> *place, and there He prayed. Mark 1:35*

Secret Place

In the Secret Place of Sacred Transformation,
change me, Lord Jesus.
Open eyes, ears, heart and soul,
and pour out Spirit and Truth.
Let holy encounter forever mark
and completely renew.
I belong to You, O King.
Yet flesh
and world
and enemy
tug and pull
and taunt—
and weariness sets in.
Let the wonder and beauty of You
spark fresh flame in my heart again today, my Lord.
Let worship define and
transform my soul.

He who dwells in the secret place of the Most High shall abide
under the shadow of the Almighty. I will say of the Lord,
"He is my refuge and my fortress; my God, in Him I will trust." Psalm 91:1-2

"But you, when you pray, go into your room, and when you have shut your door, pray to your Father who is in the secret place; and your Father who sees in secret will reward you openly." Matthew 6:6

Speak Again

Speak to me again, my King,
of the sheer wonder and joy
of Your Salvation—
of the matchless, earnest power
of the Blood that beckons
and the Name that calls.
The fire under our feet rages, Father.
Shield us from deadly flame,
and ignite, fan,
pour holy oil
on Holy Inferno.
Let the fire of heaven consume us,
refine us,
and spread as wildfire
through all our being and
all we touch.
You are our only hope.
There are no words

but Yours.

Speak again, dear King.

Speak again.

> *Restore to me the joy of Your Salvation,*
> *and uphold me by*
> *Your generous Spirit. Psalm 51:12*

> *"Lord, to whom shall we go?*
> *You have the words of eternal*
> *life." John 6:68*

Suit Up

Settle into My power, Child.
There is no strength mightier,
no force of darkness
able to overcome.
Have I not given Blood,
and Name above all names?
Do not fear, little One,
though you see the days are evil.
I shield you.
I envelope and fill you.
I give you all you need for your life.
It is well.
It is good,
because I am good,
and My mercy endures forever.
Suit up, Love.
Game on.

For God has not given us a spirit of fear,
but of power and of love
and of a sound mind. 2Timothy 1:7

Put on the whole armor of God, that you
may be able to stand against the wiles of
the devil. Ephesians 6:11

Higher Words

There are higher words than the words of man and
the accusing whispers of the enemy.
The Words of the One whose ways
are far above the flesh realm,
whose Whispers and Thunders
echo powerfully through every place,
seen and unseen...
The mighty words of The Way,
The Truth
and The Life—
of the King of Kings
and the Lord of Lords.
Those are the words that define you.
Those are the prevailing words
that will never fall to ground,
never unravel,
never be found untrue,
never cease to operate in your life.

Life words, creating words, healing words—
words of love and strength
that pierce to core
and divide the most ingrained thought,
so that Spirit and Truth prevail
in you.

> *For the Word of God is living and pow-*
> *erful, and sharper than any two-edged*
> *sword, piercing even to the division*
> *of soul and spirit, and of joints and*
> *marrow, and is a discerner of thoughts*
> *and intents of the heart. Hebrews 4:12*

Boundless

The Lord is boundless,
barred by none,
limited by nothing.
He moves through time and space,
and His Spirit fills the earth.
Angels heed His Word and His Script
echoed by your heart and tongue.
Your cries,
your prayers,
your Spirit-enabled groans move the King,
and His answers are as boundless as Himself.
No limits.
No boundaries.
No barrier of man or weapon of enemy
can intercept or interfere.
Daniel prayed,
and an angel was sent in response.
Warfare ensued,

but victory surely came.
And it will surely come for you.
Mountains melt like wax.
Angels rise to act.
Sin falls to the ground,
powerless.
Spirit fruit and divine interventions
break through into your realm.
Hallelujah!

> "For with God nothing will be impossible." Luke 1:37

Power in the Tongue

Spirit-led words strung together
become power in the heart of the hearer—
words of strength and beauty that
form an image of Christ,
the Word fleshed for us.
I surrender soul
for cleansing and refreshing,
for filling and delighting,
and out of that, Lord,
let fresh Life-words flow.
Oh, such power in the tongue—
death and life,
cursing and blessing.
I choose life.
I choose blessing.
Pour it in my heart and
out of my mouth,
mighty Holy Spirit.

"For out of the abundance of the heart his mouth speaks." Luke 6:45

Death and life are in the power of the tongue... Proverbs 18:21

Communion

I come to the Table,
with mind racing,
for holy meal.
Holy Supper,
filling my core
and settling my soul,
consuming fear and
chasing doubt.
Thank You for receiving me
at Your Table, my King.
And You Yourself serve me.
Hallelujah.
Thank You, my Lord.
Wine from holy veins.
Bread from the one and only
Giver of Life.
Sweet, tender,
powerful Communion.

144

*And He took bread, gave thanks and
broke it, and gave it to them, saying,*
*"This is My Body which is given for you;
do this in remembrance of Me."*
*Likewise He took the cup after
supper, saying,*
*"This cup is the new covenant in My Blood,
which is shed for you." Luke 22:19-20*

"I am the bread of life." John 6:48

That Voice

Oh, that Voice.
In the dark and roar of the times,
that Voice rising within core
and speaking Truth
is such treasure...
matchless.
priceless.

Take Me at My Word, Child.
I do not tease or deceive;
I do not change or waver.
Attack does not ever mean
I have deserted or declined,
but that the thing You carry
is a threat to enemy plans,
and he is furious.
You, however,
are secure.
Covered, shielded,

embraced, treasured.

All is well,

and all will be as I have spoken.

It is well.

You are well.

Rejoice,

and see the wonders

I will do.

> *"So when he spoke to me I was strength-ened..." Daniel 10:19b*
>
> *"My sheep hear My voice, and I know them, and they follow Me." John 10:27*
>
> *Law was written on Stone. Grace was written on Stone rolled away...*
> ***Thank You, Lord.***

The *King* Is *Moving*

The King is doing a work in the earth,
and you are called to be a part of it.
It is glorious.
It is full of love,
dripping with anointing,
brilliantly moving and
touching multitudes of hungry souls.
Oh, He is good.
Great is His mercy.
Don't fear darkness or evil reports—
it is simply the state of the earth
in these last days.
The Overcomer lives in you.
You are more than a conqueror.
Magnitude is coming that God alone
can produce.
Bow head.
Rejoice heart.
The King is on the move.

"Behold, I will do a new thing, now it shall spring forth; shall you not know it? I will even make a road in the wilderness and rivers in the desert." Isaiah 43:19

Kingdom Come

Oh, Father, Your Kingdom come here!
Everyone on board,
no comparisons, jealousies,
personal platforms
or selfish ambitions—
just all taking our God-appointed places,
using our Grace gifts to
encourage, lift up
and show the Beauty of the Lord.
Dark are the days and perilous the times.
It is time to arise in strength—
to radiate Love,
and employ Holy Spirit in every encounter.
Time to seek and pray and share,
and come together as
One.

There are diversities of gifts, but the same Spirit. There are diversities of ministries, but the same Lord. And there are diversities of activities, but it is the same God who works all in all. But the manifestation of the Spirit is given to each one for the profit of all...
1 Corinthians 12:4-7

John, the Beloved

John, the Beloved, exiled to Patmos by men,
was "in the Spirit on the Lord's Day."
He was found in the Spirit,
not in bitterness.
Not in abandonment.
Not refusing to worship,
because things didn't turn out like
he thought.
He was not sulking, angry or
depressed,
but was in the beauty and wonder of seeking
the Lord in Spirit and Truth.
Fellowship with Light in his darkest hour.
Quickened by Spirit
when silenced by man.
Depths of heaven given when
depths of earth were refused.
Revelation words poured out by Jesus,

when no words of man were heard.
The enemy meant to silence,
isolate and
discourage—
but the Lord used the stillness to speak Life
that would echo through eternity.
In what seemed like earthly defeat,
vast victory and matchless power words
were released.
Thank You Father!
Evil used for good.

> *I was in the Spirit on the Lord's Day, and*
> *I heard behind me a loud voice,*
> *as of a trumpet... Revelation 1:10*

I Come

I cannot stand before You in my own flesh, Lord.
I must have Your beautiful, pure, perfect covering,
Your excellent Robe of magnificent Righteousness.
I must be hidden in Christ alone,
so that Christ alone is gazed upon.
Swallowed up by radiant Light,
wrapped in Glory,
swaddled in deepest of Loves,
covered by Beauty,

spoken for by Holy Blood.
In these, my Lord,
I come before You.
So many wonders yet unopened here, My Love.
So many Beauties and Joys.
Expect them.
They are yours.

*"For you died, and your life is hidden
with Christ in God." Colossians 3:3*

A Word

I have a Word,
and the enemy has a word.
Choose this day the word that will be
engrafted into your soul.
One will bless and heal,
one will kill and destroy.
It seems such a simple choice,
but crafty is the one who deceives
and twists lies into false beauty.
Choose.

I choose You, Lord!
Please, Holy Spirit, flood and pour
and overwhelm every darkness!
Let Your Life Words quicken my core,
center my being,
release my essence and
heal my frame.

Fresh Rhema here, my King.
Fresh Words.

Choose His Word,
come into alignment,
and watch miracles unfold...

> "See, I have set before you today life and good, death and evil, in that I command you today to love the Lord your God, to walk in His ways, and to keep His commandments, His statutes, and His judgments, that you may live and multiply; and the Lord your God will bless you in the land which you go to possess."
> Deuteronomy 30:15-16

Swaddled

Blood that would defeat hell and
redeem the sons of Adam
came wrapped in tiny, swaddled
Babe.
Power greater than depths and heights,
that can break every chain,
entered earth realm confined
to mere flesh.
Praise the King of Kings,
the Lord of Lords,
Messiah, the Christ,
the Son of the Living God.
He burst through to get to you.
So precious are you.
He was swaddled so you could be
unbound.

And the Word became flesh and dwelt among us, and we beheld His glory, the glory as of the only begotten of the Father, full of grace and truth. John 1:14

Run To the *King*

I run to the Manger—
to Bethlehem—
to that place where
God entered flesh,
where earthly womb was opened
with heaven's Lamb,
where sacred Blood was delivered
through fallen vessel.
Oh, I need You so.
I love You so.
I need God to enter,
to break open,
my own flesh,
my whole realm
and let that holy Sacrifice
redeem all.

Blood bought the indescribable gift of
Holy Spirit filling, quickening, consuming.
Incorruptible Blood covers,
purifies, rebuilds—
the incorruptible working on your
corruptible.
All else falls before You, Lord.
Nothing matters but knowing You.
Beautiful King,
before You I bow.

> *And of His fullness we have all received,*
> *and grace for grace. John 1:16*

A Roar

A roar thundered in my heart as I read Isaiah 62:
"And they shall call them The Holy People, The Redeemed
of the Lord;
and you shall be called Sought Out, A City Not Forsaken."

He **will do** His work,
His good pleasure,
His delight,
His ancient, perfect plans—
even in you, Love—
even in your family—
even through your trembling hands—
even through all you have walked through.
He will not cease seeking you out,
speaking healing Truth to your soul,
pouring holy Words into earthly frame.
He will never forsake you,
never turn His back on you,
never give up on you or

refuse to unfold the Script.

Rest, Love.

He's got you.

Your devastations and desolations are not too much for His Redemption.

> "You shall also be a crown of glory in the hand of the Lord, and a royal diadem in the hand of your God. You shall no longer be termed Forsaken, nor shall your land any more be termed Desolate; but you shall be called Hephzibah, and your land Beulah; for the Lord delights in you..." Isaiah 62:3-4

Forgive

Peace cannot flow until you forgive.
Release them to the only righteous Judge.
The hard stone embedded in your
soul from their wounding
will torment and hinder you until you
forgive.
Oh, Father,
only with Your help,
*only with **Your words** embedded,*
filling, cleansing, healing,
replacing the wounds.

"Unto us a child is born…"

Us.

He came for you,
and also for those who slander, betray, mock.
He came for you,
and for the cruel, and those who
drove the knife the deepest.
Us.
Blood given for all.
The wounded and the wounder are each just
as desperate
for the touch of the King.
Let Him touch and cleanse.
Let the power of forgiveness free.
Let the perfect heart of Father deal with your
offender.
And remember...
the sin against you never defines you.
Get up!
Let the sparkling Beauty of who you really are
finally shine.

Let the radiant glory of a heart at peace
be seen upon you.
"Arise, shine, for your Light has come..."

> *...bearing with one another, and for-*
> *giving one another, if anyone has a*
> *complaint against another; even as*
> *Christ forgave you, so you also must do.*
> *Colossians 3:13*

Deal With the *Lies*

Deal with the Lies that came from the Wounds.
They are meant to defeat you.
The people they came through were just
pawns of the enemy,
aimed at shaking your core.
Forgiveness opens the door for Spirit and Truth to
set about healing, cleansing,
teaching, transforming.
Unforgiveness builds a wall,
not only between you and the offender,
but between you and the Lord.
Nothing *is worth that.*
Unforgiveness locks you in survival mode.
Forgiveness releases you to
thrive-
not just to exist,
but to grow up in the Vine and become strong,
bearing far reaching fruit.

"For if you forgive men their trespasses, your Heavenly Father will also forgive you.
But if you do not forgive men their trespasses, neither will your Father forgive your trespasses."
Matthew 6:14-15

Expect

Put language to your expectation,

your hope—

that forward look you have and live by-

because of the priceless Blood of Redemption.

In Christ, you are a new creature,

fit for a new heaven and a new earth.

You possess a great transformation,

a deep and lasting renewal,

an outpouring whose origin is the very

Throne of the Most High God.

Hallelujah!

What do you expect, then?

I expect healing, because of His stripes.

I expect fruitfulness, because of His Spirit within me.

I expect abundant life, because of His Blood.

I expect Shalom, because He is the Prince of it.

I expect renewal, because old things have passed away.

I expect foul spirits to flee, because they MUST

bow to His Name.

I expect generational curses broken and blessing released,

because He is my Father.

I expect a new identity,

because He gives a new name.

Oh, hallelujah!

Praise You, Jesus, the reason for all hope!

I expect answered prayer,

because He gives the righteousness of Christ,

and the prayer of the righteous avails much—

much power released,

much heaven called to earth,

much unseen brought into clear vision.

I expect, not with a wishing hope,

but with a strong, confident *knowing,*

and in that knowledge,

resting heart.

> *Now hope does not disappoint, because the love of God has been poured out in our hearts by the Holy Spirit who was given to us. Romans 5:5*

Can I show You

Can I show you some things, Child?
Oh, Father, **yes**.

-Praying for those who have deeply wounded you,
especially from your house and the House of God,
brings a release in your core that
sets you free from their death-words and actions.
It's part of the fullness
of forgiveness.

-Don't judge My Body based
on what a few in the
church have done.
-Holiness is a *lifestyle* of enjoying My Presence,
letting glory radiate into and through you,
rejecting overt and covert darkness,
because it cannot stay in the Light.
It flees.
"Holy" is a healthy, powerful, whole life

that abides in Christ,

that hears Throne Room whispers as you soak
in the Word,

and translates it through love to your world.

Christ in you, and you in Him,

bringing supernatural reality

into natural realm.

Being Holy is never a checklist,

never legalism.

No hint of self-righteousness in works or attitude.

It's all Him—Jesus.

And it's you enjoying

the gift of being right with God.

-Realize the glory of Christ in you. Know it. Root
deep in it. Let it flood your deepest core.

It's so, so beautiful, Child.

> *To them God willed to make known what*
> *are the riches of the glory of this mystery*
> *among the Gentiles; which is Christ in*
> *you, the hope of glory. Colossians 1:27*

Motives

Jesus didn't heal Peter's mother-in-law
so she would get up and serve Him.
*He served healing
because He so loved her,*
and she served hospitality
because she so loved Him.

Motives are everything.
*The King's motive
is always Love.*

> *Now when Jesus had come into Peter's
> house, He saw his wife's mother lying
> sick with a fever. So He touched her
> hand, and the fever left her. And she
> arose and served them.*
> *Matthew 8:14-15*
>
> *Let all that you do be done with love. 1
> Corinthians 16:14*

Welcome

Welcome, little Child.
Earth needs your gifts,
your joy, your voice,
the deep call implanted
in your soul by Father.
You are seen.
You are so, so loved.
Beauty is woven into your very being,
and there is a glorious plan.
Angels guard you;
God directs you, and
you're invited to walk with
the King of Kings.
There's so much more than you now see,
and it is good.
It is well.

*"Before I formed you in the womb
I knew you;
before you were born I sanctified you;
I ordained you as a prophet to the
nations." Jeremiah 1:5*

Friends

"I have called you friends..."
Even though...
even when...
even *then*.
The King has covenanted, cleansed and
befriended.
Arms spread wide,
head-thrown-back laughter and delight,
fellowship,
fun.
What a Friend.

So many run when crises comes.
But not this tender Friend.
The King steps in,
comes close, holds,
gathers tears,
whispers Hope.
He covers and shields in tender Mercy

and miraculously restores Joy.
And the joy of the Lord is matchless strength
infused in depths of soul.
Beautiful, Faithful Friend.

> *"No longer do I call you servants, for*
> *a servant does not know what his*
> *master is doing;*
> *but I have called you friends, for all*
> *things that I heard from My Father I*
> *have made known to you." John 15:15*

The Lord is Good

"Oh, give thanks to the Lord, for He is good!
For His mercy endures forever."
Simple declaration that releases
such magnitude of power to your soul.
Simple words,
repeated over and over again,
till they move from mouth to heart.
"He is good"—counteracts deceptions and fears
that say He isn't;
that His outpouring of goodness
stopped just short of you,
because *look at this impossible thing.*
That declaration shreds the lie that
His powerful mercy and compassion have
overlooked and skipped *your* life,
that you will never become who
you were meant to be
and that you will never fully prosper.

His Word declared tears apart the lies that
come against your heart.
He is good
to me.
His mercy endures
for my life.
He has done and yet will do mighty acts
in my heart.
And in that knowledge,
praise rises up.
Oh, give thanks to the Lord,
for He is good!

> *Oh, give thanks to the Lord, for*
> *He is good!*
> *For His mercy endures forever.*
> *Psalm 136:1*

Sweet Hour

Oh, sweet time of prayer—
set-apart time with the King,
how precious is your covering!
How deep and healing the
Spirit words poured out from You!
They swell within
and touch the deepest core,
transforming, igniting,
settling, anointing,
commissioning,
speaking Truth.
Thank You for such privilege, dear Father.
Thank You.

> *Early in the morning, having risen a*
> *long while before daylight,*
> *He went out and departed to a soli-*
> *tary place;*
> *and there He prayed. Mark 1:35*

The Fields

Look at the fields...
Every heart is yearning for Father's great, faithful,
perfect Love.
Every soul desperately needs to be
covered by the Blood of Jesus.
Every life needs the indwelling
power of the Holy Spirit.
Every
single
one.
And every heart needs a daily
infusion of fresh mercy and grace.

Love of Father,
flood us.
Blood of Son,
cover us.
Power of Spirit,
fill us.

Salvation to the uttermost;
strength to the innermost.

> *"Behold, I say to you, lift up your eyes and look at the fields, for they are already white for harvest." John 4:35*

Fragments to Baskets

All the dropped, fragmented pieces of your life
matter.
Nothing is wasted with the King.
He tenderly leads you to gather every crumb that
put together make a whole.
A whole you,
touched by abundant grace.
Divine supply given for what seemed impossible.
The situation that looked like it would cause
you to faint
becomes a *vehicle*
for the miraculous touch of God.

> So when they were filled, He said to
> His disciples, "Gather up the fragments
> that remain, so that nothing is lost".
> Therefore they gathered them up, and

*filled twelve baskets with the fragments
of the five barley loaves which were left
over by those who had eaten.*
John 6:12-13

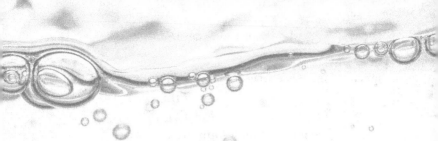

Drink

I come to drink Living Water, my Lord.
I come to lean into that wellspring of Life—
that magnificent Fountain that
never runs dry.
Quench fresh this heart, my King.
Flood my core with
Your great fullness.
Pour into me waves of pure love,
of deep joy,
of priceless peace.
All you are,
all you have for me,
funneled from Your Throne,
and flowing into and through
this little soul.
For Your glory.

"...but whoever drinks of the water that I
shall give him will never thirst.
But the water that I shall give him will
become in him a fountain of water
springing up into everlasting
life." John 4:14

I Am Working

You have not come in vain, My Child.
I am.
And I am working, arranging,
opening, closing,
releasing to you according to My
pure, perfect plans.
Much is written in the Scrolls for
your beautiful life, and
tears are simply
a backdrop for My glory.
Rejoice!
Anticipate great
joy!

> *"For I know the thoughts that I think*
> *toward you," says the Lord, "thoughts*
> *of peace and not of evil, to give you a*
> *future and a hope." Jeremiah 29:11*

Wash My Feet, Lord

Wash my feet, Lord,
for they have wandered
into murky waters.
The world has clung to them,
and flesh has justified.
I bare them before Your
presence and grace, and say,
oh, my Lord, *cleanse.*
Loose me from anything
that hinders my run,
that weighs down my dance,
that mars the beauty of Your touch.
I have turned feet and looked back,
with deep pain,
to places unfit for Kingdom.
Wash me, my Lord.
Turn radiant, pure feet then
to the direction of Your Voice,
so that never would I stray

or stumble
or walk unworthy of Call.
You are so beautiful, Lord.
Make me like You.

> *Jesus said to him, "He who is bathed*
> *needs only to wash his feet, but is com-*
> *pletely clean..."*
> *John 13:10*

The Song

I want to hear your heart song, Child.
Not talent or scripted melody,
but that sweet symphony of Love
that emanates from
your core.
I so cherish it.
I so delight in it.
I smile and draw near as
its Beauty rises.
So beautiful.
Joy set before Me.
I so love you.

> *Oh, sing to the Lord a new song! For He has done marvelous things; His right hand and His holy arm have gained Him the victory! Psalm 98:1*

Encourager

I am an encourager, Child.
Always an encourager.
Voices that tell you otherwise
are not Mine.
Discouragement
is never My strategy.
Hear My Voice through holy Script
and rejoice, again I say,
rejoice!
For it is pure,
passionate for your good,
and will lead you out of deception
and dark whispers
into abundant
Life.

Oh, Father, I ask for ears to hear!

*"I have come that they may have life, and
that they may have it more abundantly."
John 10:10*

Strength

I am Strength,
and I dwell within you,
so rise up joyously, victoriously,
in that mighty flow!
Nothing can weaken!
Enemy attempts must turn
back in defeat!
You are filled with a Strength that is
matchless, overcoming,
undefeatable and unending.
The same strength that filled Jesus as He
stood up in the tomb
now fills you.
Oh, precious Child, so often you look at flesh strength.
Look deeper.
Look up.
Astounding victory is yours forever.
As I am,

so are you,
because My Spirit floods your core
and establishes your precious steps.
Hallelujah.
Thank You, Lord.

> *...and what is the exceeding greatness of His power toward us who believe, according to the working of His mighty power which He worked in Christ when He raised Him from the dead and seated Him at His right hand in the heavenly places. Ephesians 1: 19-20*

Wealth Words

There is wealth inside you, Child.
Wealth words that will pour out
healing, hope, restoration, resurrection.
Wealth deposited from heaven's treasury,
a lavishness unmatched in the earth.
Oil flows.
Rich, pure, powerful oil.
Will the One who placed it within
not surely show you where
to release it?
You won't miss it, My Love.
The devil is a liar.
I hear chains breaking off
your heart!
Anointing is breaking every
single yoke.
Sweet, sweet freedom!
Dancing, joyful soul!

The oil will flow out and bring healing and refreshing to all who receive it.
So beautiful to Me is a heart
that pours out oil
abundantly!

> *"However, when He, the Spirit of truth, has come, He will guide you into all truth; for He will not speak on His own authority, but whatever He hears He will speak; and He will tell you things to come." John 16:13*

> *"But you have an anointing from the Holy One, and you know all things." 1 John 2:20*

> *"But the anointing which you have received from Him abides in you..." 1 John 2:27*

Jesus, Our Advocate

I am your advocate in Holy Court—
in that awesome place
where destinies are transacted,
that breathtaking place
where no sin can enter,
where divine plans are
supplied for action,
where you are commissioned
and angels commanded.
I know the accusations brought
against you,
and I know the depth of their truth.
but Blood speaks
louder, clearer, sharper.
Blood shouts, "It is finished!"
and *it is done.*
You are covered,
sheltered from the hot breath

of the father of lies.
And in that covering
you prosper.
Your gifts unfold and grow strong.
The depths of your heart
become the depths of My pleasure.
The words of your mouth
become words
echoed from My Throne.
So beautiful are you, Love,
in the reflection
of the Son.

> *My little children, these things I write*
> *to you, so that you may not sin. And if*
> *anyone sins, we have an Advocate with*
> *the Father, Jesus Christ the righteous.*
> *And He Himself is the propitiation for*
> *our sins, and not for ours only but also*
> *for the whole world. 1 John 2:1-2*

It's Time

It's time, Love.
You feel the shift,
you sense the season.
Words breathed from heaven
are forming, creating, establishing.
Joy is exploding within your soul,
for long-awaited promises are
becoming reality.
Not one cry has been
unheard.
No prayer has been
unacknowledged.
Watery tears are being turned to wine, Love,
for My touch brings miraculous
transformation.
Words will pour from heaven as a river
of golden oil—
a flowing balm of

strength and delight.
My gift to you.
My gift through you.

> *To everything there is a season, a*
> *time for every purpose under heaven...*
> *Ecclesiastes 3:1*

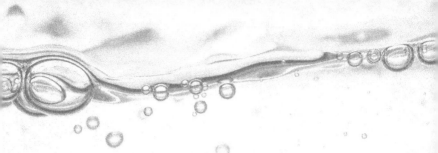

Deep to Deep

Deep to deep, Father,
speak wisdom.
Release flow of anointing,
break every yoke.
Align with Kingdom purposes,
activate heaven's plans,
fill abandonment gaps,
renew battered minds,
transform ashes to sparkling gems.
You alone, Lord,
are worthy of praise.
You alone are able to reach depths of men
with heights of heaven.
I love You, my King.
Deep words
to deep hearts.

> *Deep calls to deep at the noise of Your*
> *waterfalls... Psalm 42:7*

Cleanse Thoughts

Oh, Father, the flesh thoughts
stab and mar and
hinder the flow of Holy,
of Throne Room thoughts,
of mind of Christ,
of continual conversation with You,
the Most High.
Forgive me.
Cleanse me.
Bathe my being and
set me upright,
in sacred position,
postured to hear Your whispers
above the thunders
of earth.

...casting down arguments and every high thing that exalts itself against the knowledge of God, bringing every thought into captivity to the obedience of Christ... 2 Corinthians 10:5

Abundantly More

I long to show you My strength.
It is My great pleasure to meet you at your cries
and release to you abundantly more.
Matchless, endless wellspring of joy releases as
your cries invite My presence,
and in that place nothing shall be impossible.
You have asked for what you feel
are enormous requests.
Ask bigger.
You've only touched My hem.
So much treasure intended for you, Child.
So much beauty
from so many ashes.
The enemy has crouched near
to steal and destroy,
but you have done well to turn to Me.
I'm here.
I'm with you.

I'm working the miraculous—the divine—
in the unseen.
I will be glorified greatly through
your life.

> *"It is your Father's good pleasure to give*
> *you the Kingdom." Luke 12:32*

Boldly

Boldly approach the Throne of Grace,
where mercy and love radiate and consume,
where hearts are tendered and filled with wisdom,
where Father's delight is poured out
upon even you.
Boldly, because of Blood covering.
Boldly, because of Christ's Name
imparted to you.
Boldly, because you are now seated with Him in heavenly places.
Boldly, because you are in covenant with the Most High God,
matchless and undefeatable.
Boldly, because though enemy crouches near,
angelic defense is released and surrounds.
Boldly, because you are a new creation,
filled with Spirit of God,
marked and dressed in the purity of Christ.
Sacrifice of holy Blood speaks on altar for you.

Nothing here is impossible.
Oh, the beauty of Boldly...

> Let us therefore come boldly to the
> throne of grace, that we may obtain
> mercy and find grace to help in time of
> need. *Hebrews 4:16*

Victory

Victory of mind is victory, indeed,
  for there is the beginning of all your life.
"As a man thinks, so is he."
So is he.
Retrain those thought patterns.
Bring them into alignment
with Truth.
Present all before Me,
taking captive thoughts that
find root apart from Me,
and casting them out before
they grow and spread.
Nourish, dwell on,
keep continually before you *My* thoughts,
the very mind of Christ expressed to you in
Spirit and Truth.
That mind is victorious.
That mind is unstoppable.

That mind is free, thriving, healthy and
able to give health to others.
Victory, My love, is
yours.

> *For as he thinks in his heart, so is he.*
> *Proverbs 23:7*

You are Mine

I am the Lord,
sovereign, mighty, glorious,
unrivaled in strength, power, love.
Matchless.
You are Mine,
planned for, cherished,
with divinely-scripted plans.
Truth reigns—and reigns in you.
Delight in it.
Spread wide your hands,
lift your head,
and receive with great joy
all I have waiting for you!
It's so gloriously good,
My Love!

> *"These things I have spoken to you, that
> My joy may remain in you,
> and that your joy may be full." John 15:11*

Undergird My Heart

Undergird my heart, Father.
It cracks and leaks
and bears deep gashes.
Come to those places, Lord,
with your healing.
Deep to deep,
oil poured forth.
You alone are able.
So desperate am I for
Your fullness.
You see roots and crevices and
canyon wounds,
yet Your eyes gaze fully
on destiny prepared.
Come, Lord Jesus,
come, and
make me whole.

A bruised reed He will not break, and
smoking flax He will not quench;
He will bring forth justice for truth.
Isaiah 42:3

He sent His Word and healed them, and
delivered them
from their destructions. Psalm 107:20

Words to the Wounds

Pour Words into the wound, Lord,
for You alone have the Words of life—
the Words that live,
that are active,
that are sharper than sword,
and overrule every slander and curse.
Spirit, unleash the flood flow and
let it cover,
penetrate,
wash clean.
"Where else could we go?
You have the words of life."
Words of darkness and
words of men
be dissolved and voided by
the Words of
the Most High God.

But Simon Peter answered Him, "Lord, to whom shall we go?
You have the words of eternal life." John 6:68

Beautiful Word

Beautiful written words leap from page
as Living Word—
the very breath of God filling soul to
cleanse, heal, thrill,
delight, anticipate.
Thank You, Father, for breathing Beauty
onto the hearts of men,
so their pen would
write through the generations
into my very soul.

> *...for prophecy never came by the*
> *will of man,*
> *but holy men of God spoke as they*
> *were moved*
> *by the Holy Spirit. 2 Peter 1:21*

The Lie

Old lie came circling back.
Again, again, and again
it has assailed and tormented.
But progress has surely happened when,
instead of swallowing its sting
and feeding its misery,
it is recognized for what it is-
a *lie from the pit that*
fears God dwelling in
and rising up in you.
A lie meant to discourage and
stop you,
to cut off destiny.

Replace it now, My Love.
Speak Truth in its place.
You are more than
a conqueror.
What He has promised

He is able to perform.
He is always, always, *always*
faithful.

> *Yet in all these things we are more than conquerors*
> *through Him who loved us. Romans 8:37*

> *...casting down arguments and every high thing that exalts itself*
> *against the knowledge of God, bringing every thought into captivity*
> *to the obedience of Christ... 2 Corinthians 10:5*

Spirit and *Truth*

Truth without Spirit falls flat...
Spirit without Truth is
open to error.
But together,
stunningly beautiful.

> *"God is Spirit, and those who worship Him*
> *must worship in spirit and*
> *truth." John 4:24*

Unforgiveness

Unforgiveness is a seed.
If not plucked out immediately,
it takes root in heart
and grows exponentially into a
massive Tree of Bitterness.
How destructive is that Tree!
It will loom large,
overshadow and
defile many in its darkness.
It will negate so much good.
It will find words that release
Curse.
It will silence Blessing.
It is far more difficult to remove
a long-growing tree
than to take out a young seed.
Cleanse daily.

Guard well what grows
in your heart.

"Lord, how often shall my brother sin
against me, and I forgive him?
Up to seven times?" Jesus said to him, "I
do not say to you,
up to seven times, but up to seventy
times seven." Matthew 18:21b-22

...looking carefully lest anyone fall short
of the grace of God;
lest any root of bitterness springing up
cause trouble,
and by this many become defiled...
Hebrews 12:15

Goliath

What does it look like, Goliath,
when the Stone of Heaven,
the Name above all names,
the matchless,
most powerful force there is,
the fullness of Holy Blood
and all it holds
comes barreling through the spirit realm,
aimed perfectly at your weakest point,
ready to take your mocking, blocking,
blasphemous taunts down
with one blow?
Do you not quake?
"It is finished."
And so are you!
Your works against me and mine
are over!
You, "strongman,"

and your underling brothers
must flee,
because of Jesus' Blood.
Done.
Now, Victory,
unfold your spoils!

> *"Or how can one enter a strong man's*
> *house and plunder his goods,*
> *unless he first binds the strong man?"*
> *Matthew 12:29*

> *"You come to me with a sword, a spear,*
> *and with a javelin.*
> *But I come to you in the name of the*
> *Lord of Hosts,*
> *the God of the armies of Israel, whom*
> *you have defied. This day*
> *the Lord will deliver you into my hand..."*
> *1 Samuel 17:45-46*

Walk

Walk.
Forward motion.
One step at a time,
not based on what you see or know,
but on what Holy Spirit quickens deep within.
Not "name and claim,"
but standing on solid ground of Christ and
believing He is faithful to do
all He has spoken.
Not one word of His will fall to the ground.
Not one.
Body, soul and spirit tended to and
planned for by the King.

Ask Him for daily goals.
Write the vision;
make it plain.
Take the steps;
walk it out in faith.

Substance of things hoped for,
evidence of things not seen.
Becoming your reality.

> *For we walk by faith, not by sight. 2
> Corinthians 5:7*

> *Now faith is the substance of things
> hoped for,
> the evidence of things not seen.
> Hebrews 11:1*

In A Day

I can do it in a day, Child.
Is anything too hard for Me?
Can you name anything that is beyond
My reach?
What can I not
restore?
What darkness refuses to
flee at My Voice?
What dream have I birthed in you
that I refuse to
nurture and grow?
Trust Me, Child.
It is well.
It is coming.
Fully,
one hundred fold.

*"So I will restore to you the years that the
swarming locust has eaten,
the crawling locust, the consuming locust,
and the chewing locust..." Joel 2:25*

*"Behold, I am the Lord, the God of
all flesh.
Is there anything too hard for Me?"
Jeremiah 32:27*

Fire In Your Bones

Fire in your bones becomes
fire in your feet.
Word burning within compels you to
walk boldly,
where flesh would rather shrink back.
Out of heart mouth speaks,
and a heart burning with Spirit and Truth
will open wide to pour out
love, hope,
encouragement, Gospel-
bloody, bold, beautiful Gospel.
He is for us.
We are so,
so loved.

Then I said, "I will not make mention of
Him, nor speak anymore in His name."
But His Word was in my heart like a
burning fire shut up in my bones;
I was weary of holding it back, and I
could not. Jeremiah 20:9

I Have

Called You

I have not called you, dear Child,
to beg for crumbs and
grab on hems.
I have called you higher, deeper—
to the very place you are seated
with Me.
I have called you fully into My presence
as a child utterly loved,
receiving Salvation to the uttermost,
rising to fullness of destiny.
I have called you to walk with Me,
the Most High God,
as a precious, forever friend.
Believe Me for more than scraps.
Beautiful are My plans.

> *But God, who is rich in mercy, because*
> *of His great love with which He loved us,*
> *even when we were dead in trespasses,*
> *made us alive together with Christ*

*(by grace you have been saved), and
raised us up together, and made us
sit together in the heavenly places in
Christ Jesus... Ephesians 2:4-6*

Meditate

Meditate on My good works, Child.
Let your mind go back and
heart take anchor
in My faithfulness.
Traces of trial,
and healing that seems slow,
are not in any way evidence that I am
unfaithful,
that you are forgotten,
that plans will not unfold and
good will not come.
I am.
And I am working,
building, arranging,
fulfilling promises to you.
As you take hold of My past faithfulness,
it builds your soul to believe Me
for the next,

231

the greater,
the *glorious breakthrough*.
I am good, Child.

> *As an eagle stirs up its nest, hovers over*
> *its young, spreading out its wings,*
> *taking them up, carrying them on its*
> *wings, so the Lord alone led him,*
> *and there was no foreign god with him.*
> *Deuteronomy 32:11-12*

> *"And you shall remember that the Lord*
> *your God led you all the way*
> *these forty years in the wilderness..."*
> *Deuteronomy 8:2*

Be Encouraged

Be encouraged, Child.
I am your healer.
I am the One who
spreads back the veil
and speaks clarity and direction,
the One who goes before you and
makes straight your path.
I am the King of Kings,
and My word overrules any other...
The word of affliction, overruled.
The word of confusion, annulled.
The word of lack, cancelled.
The word of destiny, *enforced.*
The word of scripted plans, *enacted.*
My Word goes forth,
and all other words flee.
Angels attend My commands and
do works on your behalf.

Rejoice, Broken One.
I am your healer,
and I am
all things.

"So shall My Word be that goes forth
from My mouth;
it shall not return to Me void, but it shall
accomplish what I please,
and it shall prosper in the thing for
which I sent it." Isaiah 55:11

Let the word of Christ dwell in you richly
in all wisdom... Colossians 3:16a

Our Weapons

Our weapons are not carnal;
they are not of the earth realm.
They are forged in glory,
and are sure in victory.
They are not of the way of man,
but of the perfect plan of God.
Strongholds pull down as flimsy webs.
Mountains crumble and fall.
Chains break in two.
Repentance releases the grip of darkness,
and Light pours in.
His Words do not fail.

You are dressed in beauty,
mighty Sword in hand.
With every step you take,
Light goes forth and
increases your territory.
Poor and needy you have been,

but strong and mighty are you now.
Enemy does not have the Sword,
only whispers of deception.
My Word slices to shreds every dark suggestion
and raises you up in fullness of Victory—
hundred-fold kind.
Shalom.

*For the weapons of our warfare are not
carnal but mighty in God
for pulling down strongholds... 2
Corinthians 10:4*

*Finally, my brethren, be strong in the
Lord and in the power of His might.
Put on the whole armor of God, that you
may be able to stand against
the wiles of the devil. Ephesians 6:10-11*

Rest

Rest is holy, too, My Love.
Did I not consecrate Sabbath
for your body to restore,
your mind to ease,
your spirit to focus?
Do I not remember you are
formed from dust of earth and,
until your body takes on immortal,
you require rest?
Striving never pleases Me.
Overworking does good
to no one.
I am not impressed.
But I do so delight in your trust,
your cares cast into My hands,
your soul relaxing and
spirit rejoicing with faith.
I love to refill, refresh,

pour the new
into your precious vessel.
No legalism in My house, Love.
None.

> *"Come to Me, all you who labor and are*
> *heavy laden, and I will give you rest.*
> *Take My yoke upon you and learn from*
> *Me, for I am gentle and lowly in heart,*
> *and you will find rest for your souls. For*
> *My yoke is easy and My burden is light."*
> Matthew 11:28-30

Renewed

Oh, Father.
I come to the wellspring
of Living Water,
for surely my soul thirsts
for You.
Your streams of life renew me,
Your fountains wash over me and
restore my strength.
Your Word splashes,
as holy rain to desert soil,
and my spirit rejoices.
Great is Your mercy.
Wonderful is Your faithfulness.
In You, my Lord,
I find all of life.
Wash fresh today, Lord.
Nothing standing that You did not plant,
and everything growing strong

that is from Your hand.
Blessed be the Name of the Lord.

> *O God, You are my God; early will
> I seek You;*
> *my soul thirsts for you; my flesh
> longs for You*
> *in a dry and weary land where there is
> no water. Psalm 63:1*

Life

I've poured it out, My Love.
All you need for life that is
full of My touch,
My blessing,
My abundance and joy.
Life that is far, far more than
merely existing and striving-
life that rises out of ashes
and displays beauty of Essence restored.
Purpose renewed.
Vision clear.
Spirit, Soul, Body
in line with Me.
True life.
Transformed life.
Joyful life that reflects My heart.
What is godliness
but a living reflection of Me?

241

Never a list of rules and
checklists completed.
It is My Spirit filling yours,
My Word directing yours,
My love becoming yours,
so that all of your life spills out
the delight of the Most High.

> *...as His divine power has given to us all*
> *things that pertain to life and godliness,*
> *through the knowledge of Him who*
> *called us by glory and virtue... 2 Peter 1:3*

Thoughts

As a man thinks, so is he.
Uncap your thoughts.
Lose your limitations.
Circumstances and deceptions have
strapped hindering thoughts to your heart,
and they have sought to seep
into your very being.
That's not who you are.
That's not what I have told you.
I have called you royal priesthood,
friend in whom I truly delight and enjoy,
one whose life is meant to
prosper in abundance.
Loose from your soul any lesser word
and wrap yourself in Truth.
Oh, how I love you and
want to break through every wall of limitation
ever put before you!

What I break cannot be rebuilt,
and what I build
cannot be broken.
Hallelujah.

For as he thinks in his heart, so is he.
Proverbs 23:7

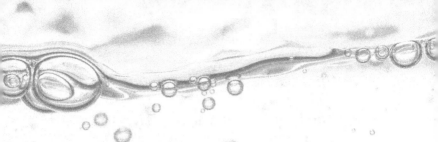

Altogether Lovely

Every facet of the King is
full of exquisite beauty,
lavish and abundant
and soaked in grace.
And, oh, the wonder-
He pours that Beauty into
every soul that will receive,
and His Spirit quickens and fills,
so that Gifts reflect
the Lovely.
All facets of His glorious Being
energizing all facets of His Body,
so that His Bride is also
altogether lovely.

"His mouth is most sweet, yes, He is alto-
gether lovely.
This is my beloved, and this is my friend,
O daughters of Jerusalem!" Song of
Solomon 5:16

The Daily

Divine, come fresh and
empower the daily.
Let the smallest task be anointed
with the greatest love,
so that even mundane
sings Your glorious praise.
Even the least desirable task
becomes woven into highest worship,
when done as unto You.
Let no part of life be left out of the flow of
Your magnificent, beautiful,
powerful touch.
All I am
given to all You are,
daily.

> *And whatever you do, do it heartily,*
> *as to the Lord and not to men...*
> *Colossians 3:23*

Holy

Holy is where My Presence is, Child.
In My Presence darkness flees,
crusty hearts become tender, fertile ground,
and deceptions crumble.
What I am pours into
all you are,
till every nook and cranny
of spirit and soul are filled
with heaven-sourced Light.
You radiate the Beauty of the Lord,
though unaware.
Oh, how beautiful holy is on you!

> *Exalt the Lord our God, and worship at*
> *His holy hill;*
> *for the Lord our God is holy. Psalm 99:9*

> *"You are the light of the world. A city that*
> *is set on a hill*
> *cannot be hidden." Matthew 5:14*

248

The Prayer

Fix our eyes on You, Father,
through power of Holy Spirit and eternal Truth,
so that the more we see,
the deeper our worship.
And in depths of worship,
let Your Kingdom unfurl into our very core,
so that Love prospers,
as it does in heaven.
Let Spirit's fruit become our definition,
and Your beautiful Name banner all.
Let Your desires become, melt into, pour out
through ours.
Give us hearts to trust Your provision and glo-
rious supply.
For who, oh Lord, is like You?
You know the need, the theft, the foolishness of our
own wisdom,
and faithful, faithful, faithful are You.
Heal us.

Shape us for Your Bread, Lord.

Blood over our sins, Father,

for apart from that magnificent covering,

who could stand?

Let that beautiful Blood and Name be our cover,

so that the matchless, gorgeous Robe of Righteousness wraps us in Beauty.

Oh, Beauty of the Lord, be upon us,

and establish the works of our hands!

Grace us also to forgive, Father, for You only are our Judge,

and bitterness will defile and destroy.

Lead us on into destiny scripted and well-planned in Your throne room,

for so much lesser seeks our attention.

Deliver us, Lord, into all Your goodness,

for dark and deadly is the evil around us.

But mighty King of Kings and Lord of Lords,

none compares to You!

No evil can ever, ever conquer You,

and no plot of wickedness can overthrow Your holy Script!

It is Your Kingdom, Your power,

Your great glory forever and ever and ever, Lord!

So be it.

"In this manner, therefore, pray: Our Father in heaven, hallowed be Your name. Your kingdom come, your will be done on earth as it is in heaven. Give us this day our daily bread, and forgive us our debts, as we forgive our debtors. And do not lead us into temptation, but deliver us from the evil one. For Yours is the kingdom and the power and the glory forever. Amen." Matthew 6:9-10

Prepared Beforehand

It's done.
Planned for, prepared,
ready and waiting for
you to walk in.
Don't fear.
Walk.
Don't depend on current vision.
Walk.
The works of God designated for your hands
are life-changing and darkness-shattering.
Believe
and walk.
Step by step,
He'll lead the way and
open the doors.
So, so good.

For we are His workmanship, created in Christ Jesus for good works, which God prepared beforehand that we should walk in them. Ephesians 2:10

For we walk by faith, not by sight. 2 Corinthians 5:7

Can I Not?

I cut covenant with Abraham
while he slept.
Can I not do in you, Wide Awake One,
all I have purposed and planned?
Can I not use what you thought was destruction
for an unimagined, glorious end?
Can I not?
Am I not able?
Is it your power that brings it about,
or Mine?
Do your questions stop My flow?
Relax and rejoice, My Love.
It is here,
even now
unfolding.

Now when the sun was going down, a deep sleep fell upon Abram... Genesis 15:12

And we know that all things work together for good to those who love God, to those who are the called according to His purpose. Romans 8:28

Grace to Grace

Oh, Holy Spirit, pour Kingdom through me!
Let all I think, do and say
be soaked in love and Truth, and
bring great courage, peace and joy.
In all my wounds pour Grace,
so that Grace flows from me to
others' scars.
On all my crusty ground
pour oil of anointing,
so that beautiful oil heals others.
Grace to grace,
in all my facets, all of Yours.
Strength to my weakness,
blessing to my strengths.
Let Your glory, Your honor, Your praise
be echoed here from
heaven's portals.

...for the kingdom of God is...righteous-
ness and peace and joy
in the Holy Spirit. Romans 14:17

"...for indeed, the kingdom of God is
within you." Luke 17:21

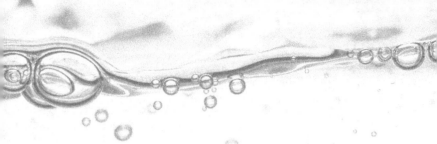

I See

I see your soul, My Love.
I see depths and core
and hidden and shadows—
the facets and intricacies and
unique beauties.
No flesh can see what I see.
I alone am the One who moves in
great compassion, wisdom and matchless power
to fully, forever restore that delightful soul...
so that no weapon formed prospers,
all that's been stolen is repaid sevenfold,
and its original intent bursts forth
in hundredfold fruitfulness.
So, so loved
are you.

For there is not a word on my tongue, but behold, O Lord, You know it altogether. You have hedged me behind and before, and laid Your hand upon me. Psalm 139:4-5

He restores my soul; He leads me in the path of righteousness
for His name's sake. Psalm 23:3

Praise

Praise Me, Love.
Praise Me even in *that,*
for praise is a great weapon
for your soul.
Praise shifts your atmosphere and
reminds you of My great,
overcoming power.
Deep worship of Me works in
the very depths of you.
You know I see.
Praise Me for what I am doing.

> Let the high praises of God be in
> their mouth,
> and a two-edged sword in their hand.
> Psalm 149:6

Tended

The Lord catches your tears and
weeps with you.
He tends your wounds,
blanketing you in
divine comfort and rest.
His very Spirit moves in
the depths of yours,
forbidding the enemy to use
pain against you.
He will minister and turn
even that for your good.
How precious it is to be
tended to by
the Most High.

> *You number my wanderings; put my*
> *tears into Your bottle;*
> *are they not in Your book? Psalm 56:8*

I Bow

I come into the place where elders bow and
angels cry, "Holy!"
where all is Light and Truth is full.
I bow with them in spirit,
and the depth of my own being cries
praise to the King.
What glorious privilege,
bought by your own pure Blood,
to find the Door open and the Way revealed
to the magnificent, matchless
Throne of the Most High God.
What honor to worship on earth's crusty soil,
even as they do in heaven.

And what is impossible here, My Love?
What can you ask of Me
that I cannot do?
What has hindered your asking?

Forgive me, Father, for unbelief.
Break the hindering and
quicken the asking,
for Your great, beautiful Name.
Your Kingdom come.

And what is My Kingdom, Love?
Think on those things,
and ask for them.

> *And I heard, as it were, the voice of a*
> *great multitude,*
> *as the sound of many waters and as*
> *the sound of*
> *mighty thundering, saying, "Alleluia!*
> *For the God Omnipotent reigns!"*
> *Revelation 19:6*

Joy of *Salvation*

Oh, the beauty of Salvation to the uttermost—
uttermost reaches of Him
poured into uttermost reaches of you.
No part untouched, overlooked,
ignored or forsaken.
Nothing impossible
or out of His sight.
Jonah was seen,
and a way of escape provided,
even in belly of whale.
Our running, hiding, fearful places
are not unseen and, thank God,
cannot run away from His reach.
He sees the questions,
the lack of understanding,
the pain, the fear.
Yet He views them through His eternal lens
and will rescue in perfect time.

And as His Salvation seeps into every part of you, what
you ran from before will
become your mission.
You can't help but speak His grace.
Salvation to Spirit, Soul and Body...
complete in Him.

> *Therefore He is also able to save to the
> uttermost those who come to God
> through Him, since He always
> lives to make intercession for them.
> Hebrews 7:25*

> *...and you are complete in Him, who is
> the head of all principality and power.
> Colossians 2:10*

The Blood

Blood came in through Babe.
Holy, pure, blood of God
that would overrule and overpower Satan's scheme
to overtake man.
Blood that brings Salvation.
Blood that sets prisoners free and
makes us children of the Most High God.
Blood that shakes heaven and earth,
poured into flesh.
Oh, the Blood.
Thank You, my King.
Dear, precious Jesus.
I receive its power,
I apprehend its goodness
and I hide myself in the
shelter of its strength.
Me and mine, Lord Jesus,

covered by
the Blood of the Lamb.

> *And the Word became flesh and*
> *dwelt among us,*
> *and we beheld His glory, the glory as of*
> *the only begotten of the Father,*
> *full of grace and truth. John 1:14*

> *And they overcame him by the blood of*
> *the Lamb and*
> *by the word of their testimony...*
> *Revelation 12:11*

Deeper

There is so much deeper, My Love.
Greater measures of wisdom,
knowledge of Christ,
glories of My Name,
revelation of Truth.
You have thrilled in the splashing,
now plumb the depths.
How great is My Word,
and how great is its power in you,
as Spirit quickens within!
You will marvel and
will see it come to pass.

> *That the God of our Lord Jesus Christ,*
> *the Father of glory, may give unto you*
> *the spirit of wisdom and revelation*
> *in the knowledge of Him: the eyes of*
> *your understanding being enlightened;*

*that you may know what is the hope of
His calling,
and what the riches of the glory
of His inheritance in the saints...
Ephesians 1:17-18*

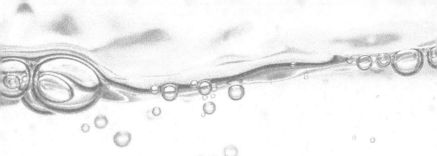

Ask

Great power lies in the asking, Child.
Strength is released as you open the door for
My Spirit and Truth to operate in your core and
penetrate your depths.
Glory is released through the asking.
Ask,
that you may receive and
that your joy may be
so full!

> *If any of you lacks wisdom, let him ask
> of God, who gives to all liberally
> and without reproach, and it will be
> given to him. James 1:5*

> *"Ask, and you will receive, that your joy
> may be full." John 16:24*

Wisdom

You desire to be wise, Child?

I am.

All wisdom is held in Me.

Come as a little child, then,

to the Master.

Come empty, to be filled.

Come willing to be taught,

shaped,

molded.

There are depths to plumb

that you know not of.

Beauties you have yet to see.

Mysteries still to unravel and

marvel in.

You have seen good...

greater still awaits!

Wisdom is the principal thing; therefore get wisdom.
And in all your getting, get understanding. Proverbs 4:7

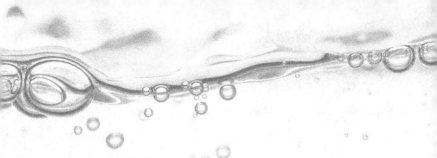

Presence

Your Presence,
weighty and
full of deep-spreading joy
and great love,
floods my soul.
Oh, thank You, my King.
Who can put eloquence to eternal?
Who can word Your wonders?
Who can describe Your delights?
Glory from heaven's realm
settling into earthen clay.
Such mystery!
Bless Your holy Name,
Lord Jesus!

> *But we have this treasure in
> earthen vessels,
> that the excellence of the power
> may be of God
> and not of us. 2 Corinthians 4:7*

Sword

Teach me to stand the Ground, Lord.
In the enemy's fury,
in the backlash sent to discourage,
weaken and destroy,
teach me to stand in Victory
already won.

The Sword, Love.
My Word is not called "Sword" for naught.
Was it not the weapon Christ used
in trial of wilderness?
It is final word,
established in heaven.
Before its power all other words
must bow.
Bring the other words before Me,
and get *My* heart on the matter.
Word Made Flesh fights and intercedes
for Word in you.

It is finished,
forever established in heaven,
and *it shall be*
as I have spoken.
Father of Lies wants to
hinder your faith and vision,
so you will remain stuck and
the beautiful, unfolding plans
will be cut off.
I am the finisher,
and you know well I'm the Author.
I have the final word.
Be glad, My Love.
Rejoice in finished work unfolding.

> *But He answered and said, "It is written..." Matthew 4:4*

> *Therefore He is able to save to the uttermost those who come to God through Him, since He always lives to make intercession for them. Hebrews 7:25*

> *Therefore take up the whole armor of God, that you may be able to withstand in the evil day, and having done all, to stand. Ephesians 6:13*

Victory

Victory *is* yours, Child.
It really is.
You are seated with Me in
heavenly realms,
in the place of ruling and reigning,
in the place where
all is enveloped by and
hidden in Christ.
Impenetrable armor surrounds you.
You command victory from that place.
You don't battle *for* victory,
you battle *from* victory.
The enemy, you well know,
is bent on deceiving and stealing,
on blinding you to who you are
and what you have,
and what you have full access to,
so that he can gain legal right to destroy.

Blood bought back every legal right.

He is trespassing.

You may use the Matchless Name that defeated him, and resist.

Thank You, thank You,
my Father.

> *For if by the one man's offense death reigned through the one, much more those who receive abundance of grace and of the gift of righteousness will reign in life through the One, Jesus Christ. Romans 5:17*
>
> *For you died, and your life is hidden with Christ in God. Colossians 3:3*
>
> *...and raised us up together, and made us sit together in the heavenly places in Christ Jesus... Ephesians 2:6*

Come As A Child

Have I not always seen you, My Love?
I remember when you were just a little child…
you brought Me such joy!
I knew your path and steps,
and it was with great delight that
I opened doors.
Yes, *even then,*
the enemy sought to hinder and
deceive and destroy,
but I used it to strengthen and
deepen you.
You were so precious to Me,
as your child thoughts were pure, amazed,
eager and fearless.
Even then I filled your mind.
Do I not say, "Come as a child?"
Come continually with a mind
I have purified and filled—

eager, fearless,
in awe and wonder.
I so love you,
My little Child.

"Therefore whoever humbles himself as
   this little child
   is the greatest in the kingdom of heaven."
Matthew 18:4

"Before I formed you in the womb I knew
   you..." Jeremiah 1:5

Feelings

I cannot surrender to feelings.
Feelings don't forgive.
Feelings don't usher in Grace
and pour kindness on the wounds.
Feelings are self-protective, defensive,
bitter, vengeful, walled…
I surrender.
I submit to You, Most High God.
I resist enemy suggestions and reminders
and fix my gaze upward.
Have Your way, Lord,
and strengthen my heart
to obey.

Flesh ground is like quicksand,
pulling you in,
trapping in miry mess.
I'm calling you higher, Child.
I have so much more for you

than that.
Take My hand.
I'll lead you out to
beautiful, firm,
magnificently higher ground.
And forgive—
don't carry *their* sin
in *your* spirit.

> *Therefore submit to God. Resist the devil*
> *and he will flee from you. James 4:7*

> *Then Peter came to Him and said,*
> *"Lord, how often shall my brother sin*
> *against me,*
> *and I forgive him? Up to seven times?"*
> *Jesus said to him, "I do not say to you,*
> *up to seven times, but up to seventy*
> *times seven." Matthew 18:21-22*

Water to Wine

Bring your jars full of earth water—
your flesh tears—
and let the Master transform them
to deep wells of sweetest,
holy wine...
bringing joy, awe,
wonder and praise
at the works of His hand.

> When the master of the feast had tasted
> the water that was made wine...he said
> to him, "Every man at the beginning
> sets out the good wine, and when the
> guests have well drunk, then the inferior.
> You have kept the good wine until now!"
> John 2: 9-10

You number my wanderings; put my tears into Your bottle; are they not in Your book?
Psalm 56:8

For You, Lord, have made me glad through Your work; I will triumph in the work of Your hands. Psalm 92:4

Occupy

Teach me to occupy till You come, Lord!
To be about Your beautiful business,
looking ahead,
eyes fixed on You,
mind renewed with Truth,
power from Holy Spirit flowing and
directing every word and step.
All things new—
all things *You.*
All things of all of life occupied by and for
Your glorious Kingdom.
And what joy to hear
"Well done!"
in Your holy presence.

> "So he called ten of his servants, deliv-
> ered to them ten minas,
> and said to them, 'Do business till I
> come.'" Luke 19:13

I've Got You

I've got you, Child.
You don't have to wonder if I am
overlooking the attacks coming against you,
or if I have heard your pleas but
refused to help.
Am I not always good and
full of pure love for You?
I do see, My Love.
I see,
and My timing is perfect.
My aid is sure.
My steadfast faithfulness to you
unfailing.
I do not send destruction,
but promise to turn it and
use it for your good.
The devil is a liar,
and the father of lies.

You are whole in Me.
You are well,
and it is finished.
Rejoice,
and expect miracles to manifest
and My Word to go forth,
accomplishing more than
you dared dream.

> *Then she called the name of the Lord*
> *who spoke to her,*
> *You-Are-The-God-Who-Sees (El Roi)...*
> *Genesis 16:13*

I'm

Pouring Out

Oh Child, I'm pouring out.
Beauty of the Lord will
soak dry ground.
Wonders will unfold
from My hand alone.
My love will manifest fresh,
and *you will know it.*
"Behold, I do a new thing,
even now it springs forth!"
Ancient of Days in fullness of time,
pouring manifested Glory
that will cover the earth.
Rise!
Shine!
Get ready!
It will not pass you by.

"'And it shall come to pass in the last days," says God,
"that I will pour out of My Spirit on all flesh..."' Acts 2:17

"Behold, I will do a new thing, now it shall spring forth;
shall you not know it? I will even make a road in the wilderness
and rivers in the desert." Isaiah 43:19

Much Required

Much has been required of you, Love,
because there is much to give—
not only *to* you,
but *through* you.
You have suffered long in trial and test,
but, Child,
I do not smell smoke.
You are not destroyed—
nor even singed.
You are instead strengthened,
lifted into realms that comfort
would never have taken you.
Oh, I do so love you.
You are running well,
and best is yet to come!
Affliction has brought release,
not crippling,
and it is now healed so that

your strong feet may run in
exuberant joy!

> "For everyone to whom much is given,
> from him much required;
> and to whom much has been com-
> mitted, of him they will ask the more."
> Luke 12:48

> ...and they saw these men on whose
> bodies the fire had no power;
> the hair of their head was not singed nor
> were their garments affected,
> and the smell of fire was not on them.
> Daniel 3:27

He Passed Over

I have something for you, Child.
Something so delightful,
so pure,
full of such beauty.
I withhold no good gift from you, My Love.
It's such pleasure for Me to give to you,
even Kingdom.
It is the voice of the Liar that says
you have been overlooked,
given less,
passed over...
Oh, no!
I passed over from death to life,
so you can enjoy all of Me,
and all I possess.
Just receive, Love.
No works,
so none can boast.

Run!
Dance!
Enjoy!
Sing a new song!
You are healed,
and healing you shall see!
Hallelujah!
So be it, Lord!!!

"Do not fear, little flock, for it is your
Father's good pleasure
to give you the kingdom." Luke 12:32

Glorious Cover

Oh Father,
I come under the shelter and shadow of Your wing,
Your glorious cover,
that beautiful place where I am hidden in Christ.
I anchor my heart here,
and ask for Your outpouring.
I come boldly, by Blood,
and ask for Your touch of healing, favor,
blessing, open doors, divine appointments,
all of destiny unfolding,
unhindered.
The enemy is cruel and crafty, Lord, and
seeks our destruction.
I bow before Your throne and ask that
no weapon against us prospers,
and that every attack be turned back,
powerless.
Expose any darkness and

release magnificent light—
the light of wisdom, revelation,
knowledge of Jesus Christ.
The light of joy, of wholeness,
of victory tasted.
Light that floods heaven
and eliminates need for lamp,
come, flood here.
Let us come to life
in Your beautiful Light, Lord.

> *He who dwells in the secret place of*
> *the Most High*
> *shall abide under the shadow of the*
> *Almighty. Psalm 91:1*

Cleanse

Cleanse my motives, Lord,
root and core.
My heart will deceive me.
It will puff up and blind.
I so want to honor You, my King,
with purity and passion that is
fully sanctified—
full of Your Word alone.
You are so, so beautiful.
Let nothing of me mar
Your reflection here on earth.
Oh, my Father, Your Kingdom come—
so breathtakingly gorgeous,
full of such deep love—
and let Your mighty mission manifest
even here.
Even in me, Lord.
Even in me.

"The heart is deceitful above all things, and desperately wicked; who can know it?" Jeremiah 17:9

"Your kingdom come. Your will be done on earth as it is in heaven." Matthew 6:10

It Is Finished

It is finished…and it has begun.
Generational curses are finished,
and every lie they passed down-
wandering, affliction, addictions,
unmet potential, hindrances,
foul spirits' operations against you are done,
and their power revoked by holy,
beautiful Blood.
Hallelujah!
Every dark stronghold turned over and exposed,
like the money changers' tables.
Every weak place,
long taken advantage of,
covered over and strengthened
by the very hand of the Most High God.
Every divinely-planted gift and holy purpose
brought forth with great joy,
to be partaken of and shared,

to build glorious Kingdom.
Wrong thinking and dark deceptions cut off,
and Truth stretching deep roots in hearts,
bringing magnificent branches forth,
bearing much fruit and
giving other hearts shade to rest in.
Oh, the precious, matchless,
powerful Blood of Jesus!
Thank You, dear King.

> *So when Jesus had received the sour*
> *wine, He said, "It is finished!"*
> *And bowing His head, He gave up His*
> *Spirit. John 19:30*

> *Then He who sat on the throne said,*
> *"Behold, I make all things new."*
> *Revelation 21:5*

I Am Good

I am good, Love.
Believe Me for good.
Oh, how lies have long tried
to strangle hope,
to quench expectation,
to chase away dreams.
I overrule them all.
I see their root,
even unknown to you.
Can I not heal all?
Is anything impossible to Me, Child?
Can you name what I cannot do?
Well, then.
I am unfolding plans long established in the heavenlies
and now well prepared to enter your realm—
earth realm,
your world lit on fire with My plans and Presence.
Last ditch efforts of enemy to stop them

will always fail.
Great, great, great are My plans,
and **I will prevail.**
Do not fear,
you are supplied,
and I will never fail you.
Never will I abandon you to
figure it out on your own.
I have said,
and I will do.

> *Oh, give thanks to the Lord, for He is good!*
> *For His mercy endures forever.*
> *Psalm 136:1*

> *"For I know the thoughts that I think toward you," says the Lord,*
> *"thoughts of peace and not of evil, to future and a hope." Jeremiah 29:11*

Resurrection Power

Oh, Resurrection Power!
Matchless, magnificent,
very present power.
Time of need pulls on its grace and strength,
yet never does it diminish, dim,
fade, or pass you by.
The dangling and the dead,
both made new and glorious when
touched by its awesome might.
It lifted Messiah from grave,
and will lift you as well,
into radiant, forever Life—
free of fear,
full of victory's joy and
greatly used to build Kingdom.
So be it, Lord.
So be it.

...and what is the exceeding greatness of His power toward us who believe, according to the working of His mighty power which He worked in Christ when He raised Him from the dead and seated Him at His right hand in the heavenly places, far above all principality and power and might and dominion, and every name that is named, not only in this age but also in that which is to come. Ephesians 1:19-21

God is our refuge and strength, a very present help in trouble. Psalm 46:1

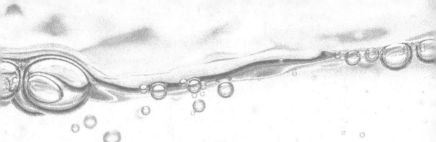

Red Sea

Remember how the sea parted, Child?
The Red Sea,
and yours.
Don't let the next challenge cause you to forget!
I have moved mountains,
parted seas,
crushed boulders and
performed miracles,
known and unknown,
on your behalf.
And I call you to move from
glory to glory and strength to strength—
from victory to
sweet, *sweet victory*.
I do not retreat, and in Me
neither shall you.
I *always* bring victory,
and beauty always rises from ashes.
*Let what needs to burn, **burn.***

And watch Me do the mighty
for you.

> *So the children of Israel went into the
> midst of the sea on the dry ground...
> Exodus 14:22*

> *But we, with unveiled face, beholding as
> in a mirror the glory of the Lord,
> are being transformed into the same
> image from glory to glory,
> just as by the Spirit of the Lord. 2
> Corinthians 3:18*

Strategy

My Word is holy strategy, Child—
the battle plan and the sure victory.
Words of others will fall,
but My Word will never fail,
return void
or be overruled.
It is weapon,
and it is healer.
It is sharp Sword
and soothing Balm.
It is forever for you,
established in heaven
and brought to earth in power
through *your mouth*.
Believe it in heart
and speak it from lips.
It will heal you and
change your very atmosphere.

*For the Word of God is living and pow-
erful, and sharper than any two-edged
sword, piercing even to the division of
soul and spirit, and of joints and marrow,
and is a discerner of the thoughts and
intents of the heart. Hebrews 4: 12*

*And take the helmet of salvation, and the
sword of the Spirit,
which is the Word of God...
Ephesians 6:17*

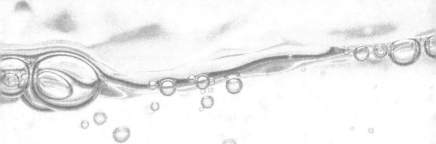

Come, Child

Come, Child, let Me gather you up.
Let Me hold you close
and just enjoy your presence.
Rest your heart—
you don't have to know all right now.
I am always faithful,
and you can fully trust Me.
Fully.
Spirit, Soul and Body.
You and your house.
I have a song to
sing over you now...

> "The beloved of the Lord shall dwell in
> safety by Him,
> who shelters him all the day long; and
> he shall dwell
> between His shoulders."
> Deuteronomy 33:12

307

The Lord your God in your midst, The
Mighty One, will save;
He will rejoice over you with gladness,
He will quiet you with His love,
He will rejoice over you with singing."
Zephaniah 3:17

...and your praise becomes a beautiful symphony
as it blends with Father's song of rejoicing over you,
joining the holy chorus being sung before the Throne
and causing inexpressible joy to break forth among all.

Thank You

Thank You for Covenant Blood, Father,
that covers, envelopes,
cleanses, renews,
transforms us into Beauty.
Thank You for its matchless power,
strength, and majesty that
floods our hearts
and burns holy flame within.
Thank You for the Door opened
by its sacrifice,
opening mystery and glory
to mere flesh and blood.
Oh, how You love the sons of men!
How You delight to show Yourself strong!
Come, Holy Spirit,
reveal more and more here,
where we long for You.
Glorify Jesus, as You desire to do.

Open eyes and ears,
and make straight the path for destiny's unfurling.
Joy.
Peace.
Delight.
Thank You, dear King.

> *...and by Him to reconcile all things to Himself, by Him, whether things on earth or things in heaven, having made peace through the Blood of His Cross. Colossians 1:20*

> *In Him we have redemption through His blood, the forgiveness of sins, according to the riches of His grace. Ephesians 1:7*

Beautiful Accounts

Oh, Jesus,
holy Script pours out beautiful accounts of
Your precious feet walking into
the darkness of man,
into circumstances that crippled, blinded,
tortured bodies and souls,
and doing the works *You alone can do.*
You are forever the same
and forever faithful.
So I ask You, dear King of Glory,
to enter into *our* circumstances,
our hearts and homes,
our bodies and soul realms,
and do the works *You alone can do.*
We so love you, dear King.

*And Jesus went about all Galilee,
teaching in their synagogues,
preaching the gospel of the kingdom,
and healing all kinds of
sickness and all kinds of disease among
the people. Matthew 4:23*

*And there are also many other things
that Jesus did which
if they were written one by one, I sup-
pose that even the
world itself could not contain the books
that would be written. John 21:25*

*Jesus Christ is the same yesterday, today,
and forever. Hebrews 13:8*

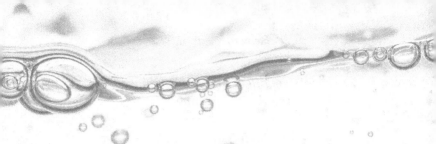

I See

I see, Child!

I am not blind to what is

veiled from your eyes.

I see ahead,

and My goodness and mercy surround you.

Do not fear, Love…

don't be afraid.

Plans are scripted with great joy,

and all the enemy sent to tear down and destroy with

will be supernaturally woven into

a beautiful song of love.

Even that.

Even for you.

I have not forgotten or forsaken you

or your house.

Rest in My pure heart for you.

*Surely goodness and mercy shall follow
me all the days of my life;*

*and I will dwell in the house of the Lord
forever. Psalm 23:6*

Unfurl

Word of God cuts through noise and fluff of
world chatter,
slicing nonsense and interference,
revealing the power of the ages given to mankind
through the Breath of God.
Holy flame burned on hearts of men and scripted
into Sword,
matchless and undefeatable.
Angels listen for it,
standing ready to implement all.
Demons tremble and flee before Word of Words,
as it will crush and annihilate them if they do not.
It is a mighty tower,
lifting higher and allowing divine Light to satu-
rate souls.
It is His will,
His promise,
His wisdom,
His delight.

It is narrow, because what can stand as its equal?
And yet it stretches broad and beautiful,
making room for all who will simply receive.
Oh, Word of God,
Word made flesh,
Sword of our strength and Giver of faith,
our defense, our architect,
our builder and deepest stream.
Oh precious Word,
unfurl your fullness here.

> *For the word of God is living and powerful, and sharper than any two-edged sword, piercing even to the division of soul and spirit, and of joints and marrow, and is a discerner of the thoughts and intents of the heart. Hebrews 4:12*

> *And the Word became flesh and dwelt among us, and we beheld His glory, the glory as of the only begotten of the Father, full of grace and truth. John 1:14*

> *And of His fullness we have all received, and grace for grace. John 1:16*

Keep Coming

Oh, Child,
when you falter and fall,
when words are careless and
stem from bitter root,
I do not leave.
Never do I forsake.
I convict,
so I may heal and
fully, abundantly restore.
I know your weakness,
and I know your heart's desire.
Just keep coming to the Fountain of Mercy,
the Throne of Grace,
for there is always found there
help for your deepest need.

> *Let us therefore come boldly to the*
> *throne of grace,*
> *that we may obtain mercy and find grace*
> *to help in time of need. Hebrews 4:16*

Flow

Flow into the deepest places, Water of the Word,
flow of Holy Spirit,
and do the cleansing and soothing
You alone can do.
Tend to what I cannot see.
Heal what has long leaked pain.
Restore all enemy has stolen and
regenerate all into strength, beauty, health.
I bring Your matchless Blood against
every trace of curse.
Release blessing, Lord.
Speak words of life that overcome.

> *...that He might sanctify and cleanse*
> *her with the*
> *washing of water by the Word...*
> *Ephesians 5:26*

*"...but the water that I shall give him will
become in him
a fountain of water springing up into
everlasting life." John 4:14*

*"And it shall come to pass in the last
days," says God,
"that I will pour out of My Spirit on all
flesh..." Acts 2:17*

Sons

Sons of Adam become sons of God
through the beautiful, pure blood of the Son—
Jesus, the Christ,
Lamb slain from the foundation of the world.
By the power of the Son
nothing is impossible to you.
Nothing!
You house the heartbeat of the Most High,
and in your surrender
He is able to rise within and
do divine and holy works
through your redeemed vessel.
Thank You, dear Father.
Thank You.

> *But as many as received Him, to them*
> *He gave the right*
> *to become children of God, to those who*
> *believe in His name. John 1:12*

Dream

What are your dreams, Child?
Have you yet dared voice them to Me?
Do they seem selfish
because *you* are in them,
because they are yours?
Do I Myself not plant dreams
in the heart of man?
Dream larger than you have deemed appropriate,
because God-dreams are larger than
your wildest expectations.
A heart set free
is a heart free to dream.
Give Me permission to
blow your mind.

> *When the Lord brought back the cap-*
> *tivity of Zion,*
> *we were like those who dream.*
> *Psalm 126:1*

Power

I've released to you so much power, Child!
Beautiful, life-changing,
Kingdom-building power from heaven
that shakes the earth.
Power of Holy Blood,
given to bloodline of man.
Power that overrules enemy accusations
and releases Light of destiny.
Power to move forward—
unstuck,
released from all
that has tormented and held back.
Power to speak and see mountains move.
Overcoming, matchless power given for all you need.
Spirit's power, entrusted to mere flesh—
gifted by Blood,
enforced by Name.
Be full, Child,

and *go forth in the strength*
of My power!

> "But you shall receive power when the
> Holy Spirit has come upon you;
> and you shall be witnesses to
> Me..." Acts 1:8

> "For assuredly I say to you, whoever says
> to this mountain, 'Be removed and cast
> into the sea,' and does not doubt in his
> heart, but believes that those things he
> says will be done, he will have whatever
> he says." Mark 11:23

Your Words

Your words, Child.
Guard so well what you allow to come forth
into your atmosphere,
your realm of influence.
So much power is laced within them—
infinitely more than you know!
Settle into Me.
Lean into My heart.
Let Spirit and Truth renew your mind
and transform your very soul.
And as you do,
the words you utter will originate in My heart,
take root and grow in yours,
and be released to bring about beautiful, pure,
healing, holy works of love.
I will move mightily through your words.
My Kingdom comes,
My will is done,

riding on your
words.

> "A good man out of the good treasure
> of his heart brings forth good; and an
> evil man out of the evil treasure of
> his heart brings forth evil. For out of
> the abundance of the heart the mouth
> speaks." Luke 6:45

My Word

My Word is living and active and
sharper than double-edged sword.
And that Word is **for you.**
What does it cut away but
that which could destroy?
What does it slice except
deceptions and strongholds?
What does it sharpen and prune but
that which will rise up strong in you,
the Truth that will heal you and
build My glorious Kingdom?
My Word brings you fresh, beautiful,
whole life as it settles deep in heart
and manifests in earth realm.
Out of heart mouth speaks,
and mighty are the utterances that
come forth from My Spirit and My Truth,
falling like refreshing, sweet rain,

healing as warm, nourishing oil,
silencing foe and giving voice to
powerful praise.
Child, ***I am My Word.***
Stay in it.

> *What then shall we say to these things?*
> *If God is for us, who can be against us?*
> Romans 8:31

Believe

Why do you beg and plead for
what is already yours, Child?
Why do you think crumbs are your portion
and lack is your lot?
Why do you wonder if the fullness of My table
is truly, truly, truly available for *you* to enjoy?
Could it be doubt, My Love?
Could it be a tiny trace of unbelief that
opens up your life to great theft?
Feelings and inadequacies matter not.
All under Blood,
as you cast them there.
Do I not say to ask,
that you may receive?
Are your requests bold and specific,
or do they quiver with wondering?
Do not be afraid, Child.
Only believe.

"Do not fear, little flock, for it your Father's good pleasure to give you the kingdom." Luke 12:32

"Do not be afraid; only believe." Mark 5:36

Expect

Expect greatness.
Greatness of the One True God,
living, moving, quickening,
guiding, speaking,
healing from within.
Greatness of greatest Words,
greatest Love,
greatest Joy,
operating in the greatest depths of your being.
Greatness of holy plans
delightfully unfolding.
Greatness of victory over all
that has come against to oppress.
Greatness of I AM, saying that in Him, you are...
more than you knew or
dared dream,
for His glorious
Kingdom come.

"Most assuredly, I say to you, he who believes in Me,
the works that I do he will do also; and greater works
than these he will do, because I go to my Father." John 14:12

Praise

Oh, Child, don't you sense it?
How praise ushers in
My mighty Presence?
How it floods your depths as you
set your gaze,
fix your heart,
and let your mouth speak what dwells in Mine?
Do you consider how unseen realm responds
as you lift up and I bow low?
Angels join in and rejoice,
and are sent on missions of victory.
Demons tremble and flee.
I fill every space within you,
and My Spirit speaks love, peace, direction…
Oh, how powerful is your heart
tuned to Mine!

Oh, Father, beautiful King,
in Your presence is fullness of joy,

and joy causes even deeper praise
to echo in depths of soul.
Peace settles into every nook and cranny.
Vision turns to Kingdom.
Gifts become a beautiful offering gladly given
for your great purposes.
Hallelujah!
Praise Your holy Name
and marvelous grace!

> *But You are holy, enthroned in the*
> *praises of Israel. Psalm 22:3*
>
> *You will show me the path of life; in Your*
> *presence is fullness of joy;*
> *at Your right hand are pleasures forever-*
> *more. Psalm 16:11*

Abundance

What does abundance look like, Child?
Surely so much more than physical provision.
Is it not gifts being used,
overflowing in fullness of purpose?
Is it not love saturating all,
washing away unforgiveness and
planting Grace deep within?
Is it not joy that defies whatever
darkness enemy suggests?
Is it not such great peace that
it passes understanding?
Could it be an outpouring,
a great release of the flow of My Spirit,
bringing wisdom, revelation,
knowledge of Christ?
Will these pure things not purify you,
and open door to greater blessing?
I've got it, Love.

Such depths of abundance coming
to you and your house!

> *"The thief does not come except to steal,*
> *and to kill, and to destroy.*
> *I have come that they may have life, and*
> *that they may have it*
> *more abundantly." John 10:10*

Beautiful

Beautiful are the works of My hand, Love.
Beauty that transcends earth's most glorious moments,
that pours heaven's joys on earth's crusty soil.
Beauty of transformation, renewal,
restoration, retribution.
Beauty of prophetic becoming words you walk in,
unfolding more than you dared dream.
Beauty of Light filling, surrounding,
clothing what was once dark.
Beauty of plans well laid by Me,
and well walked by you.
So, so beautiful are you, Love—
a precious work
of My hand.

> *And let the beauty of the Lord our God*
> *be upon us,*
> *and establish the work of our hands for us;*
> *yes, establish the work of our hands.*
> *Psalm 90:17*

Resurrection

Power of Resurrection,
released to you.
Look up!
Let Me steady your feet to
walk in it.
Holy Spirit pouring out,
filling up, overflowing and
bringing radiant life to what was stone cold, hopeless...
Strength that exists in no other place
rushing into your weakness,
flooding Despair with expectant Joy
and bringing vision to the blinded.
What crushed,
discouraged,
blinded you, Child?
What sought to steal gifts and calling?
What was put in front of you to
attempt to trip you,
weaken you,

destroy all hope?
My power, My Resurrection strength,
overrules.
Power to rise up and above—
and to become...

> *...and what is the exceeding greatness of His power toward us who believe, according to the working of His mighty power which He worked in Christ when He raised Him from the dead and seated Him at His right hand in the heavenly places... Ephesians 1:19-20*

Vital Part

You are a *vital part* of Kingdom.

A king. A priest.

Precious, holy are you!

Royalty that ministers,

chosen to do the works of the Most High

on the earth.

Your life,

bringing His Kingdom into earth realm.

Declare a thing!

Line up with the Word,

and will angels not attend

to bring it to pass,

and does all of heaven not back it up?

What, then, is out of your reach?

What cannot be done?

Walk in the beauty of

who you really are!

But you are a chosen generation, a royal priesthood, a holy nation, His own special people, that you may proclaim the praises of Him who called you out of darkness into His marvelous light...
1 Peter 2:9

Bless the Lord, you His angels, who excel in strength, who do His Word, heeding the voice of His Word. Psalm 103:20

No Limitations

There is no limitation on My Power.
It is you who limits through unbelief.
You gaze through flesh eyes and
let your expectations be capped
by what you know.
Oh, Child, man's words are not My words.
Man's resources are not My resources.
What they say is incurable and impossible
is absolutely available
through My Name and Blood.
I'm teaching you, Love.
You will see the miraculous.
Wonders will unfold as
I do what only I can.
No flesh can boast.
No man can glory.
It is My power,

imparted to you,
resurrecting the impossible.

> "For with God nothing will be impossible." Luke 1:37

Shelter of His *Shadow*

Oh, what a beautiful place, Child,
is the shelter of My shadow.
Drawn near, nestled in, secure...
so full are you here.
In that closeness,
you hear My every whisper.
My line of vision becomes
your own gaze.
My heart beats in rhythm with yours,
and yours with Mine.
Father and Child.
Groom and Bride.
Spirit to Spirit.
Matchless, precious,
indescribable Love.

> *He who dwells in the secret place of*
> *the Most High*
> *shall abide under the shadow of the*
> *Almighty. Psalm 91:1*

A New Thing

Oh, child,
I'm pouring out.
Beauty of the Lord will
soak dry ground.
Wonders will unfold,
from My hand alone.
My love will manifest fresh,
and you will know it.
"Behold, I do a new thing,
even now it springs forth!"
Ancient of Days in fullness of time
pouring manifested glory that
will cover the earth.
Rise,
shine,
get ready.
It will not pass you by.

"Behold, I will do a new thing, now it shall spring forth;
shall you not know it? I will even make a road in the wilderness
and rivers in the desert." Isaiah 43:19

Fully

Fully, love.
You are fully covered,
fully cloaked,
fully cleansed,
fully Mine.
My Word is in full operation in you,
doing more in unseen places
than you can imagine.
Oh, child,
those words reach far and wide and
will sweep through generations,
rebuilding, transforming,
setting upright,
establishing destiny.
Stay in My Word...
it is fully yours and will
fully usher in My move.

I will greatly rejoice in the Lord, my soul shall be joyful in my God; for He has clothed me with the garments of salvation, He has covered me with the robe of righteousness..."
Isaiah 61:10

For the Word of God is living and powerful, and sharper than any two-edged sword, piercing even to the division of soul and spirit, and of joints and marrow, and is a discerner of the thoughts and intents of the heart." Hebrews 4:12

Fit For His

Presence

Blood of Christ makes me fit for Your Presence, Father,
enabled to be presented to You as Your precious child–
pure, sparkling,
delightfully clean, fragrant,
drenched in Your beauty.
It covers my failures and iniquities,
and washes away darkness and tears.
It answers the enemy's legal accusations against me,
and forces him to release his death grip.
It is my strength,
my answer,
my everything.
It is my life,
my Door,
my Destiny.
It is the singular source of victory,
the only cry that brings power and change,
that truly bears the strength to transform.
It is my connection to You, Father.

It has claimed me and
changed my bloodline.
Thank You, Father, from the core of all I am.
I apply its power now, my Father,
to spirit, soul, and body,
to family,
future,
and forever plans of God for us.
No weapon formed against us may prosper as
Blood disarms,
and impossibilities bow before the Divine.
All glory, honor, and worship to You alone, King Jesus.

> *And they overcame him by the Blood
> of the Lamb and by the word of their
> testimony,*
> *and they did not love their lives to the
> death. Revelation 12:11*

Humbled

Ancient of Days who cut the ancient path,
unchanging, immovable,
the same yesterday, today, and forever,
Who Is, Who Was, and Who Is To Come-
before Your beautiful Presence, my Lord,
I bow.
Forgive us for trying to fit You into our image,
for claiming You evolve with the changing times and
the whims of men's hearts,
for imagining You condone the iniquity we cherish.
Oh, Father,
Almighty God,
wash us pure,
cleanse our feet,
set us upright in the way we are to go.
Blood of Jesus, speak for us.
Spirit and Truth, cover and flood our souls.
As we are surrendered,

lift us up.

For Your glory.

> *"If My people who are called by My Name will humble themselves, and pray and seek My face, and turn from their wicked ways, then I will hear from heaven, and will forgive their sin and heal their land."* 2 Chronicles 7:14

> *"Stand in the ways and see, and ask for the old paths, where the good way is, and walk in it; then you will find rest for your souls." Jeremiah 6:16*

Hand To Plow

Hand to plow, forward motion,
expecting seeds sown in freshly tilled soil
to grow strong in healthy, well-watered ground.
Plowing through Word,
turning Truth over,
allowing it to nurture, encourage,
water, cleanse, convict.
Plowing in prayer,
continually coming to Father,
asking for His Word to prosper
in your circumstances.
Plowing through territory meant for your gifts,
depositing excellence that honors the King.
Plowing through flesh thoughts,
taking them captive,
casting them aside as weeds to soul.
Plowing brings forth purpose.
Destiny long scripted, the very plans of God

for a future and hope,
for your part of building Kingdom,
come forth into your realm
as you move forward.
Don't look back.
What is behind you but
all that needed redemption?
What could going back bring but
hindrance,
unmet potential,
and unfulfilled plans?
Look ahead.
Press on.
Beautiful, bountiful harvest waits.

> *But Jesus said to him, "No one, having put his hand to the plow, and looking back, is fit for the Kingdom of God." Luke 9:62*

> *And He said, "The Kingdom of God is as if a man should scatter seed on the ground, and should sleep by night and rise by day, and the seed should sprout and grow, he himself does not know how...". Mark 4:26-27*

In The

Secret Place

*Unspeakable privilege to be invited to dwell in
the secret place of the Most High.*
That holy place of matchless Beauty that is
fully illumined by His Presence,
where wisdom and knowledge are rooted deep
and caused to prosper,
where all that is not of Him falls away,
where the mantle of anointing is
wrapped around your royal shoulders,
where commissioning is given and
instruction is received,
where the Word made flesh
imparts Word in you.
A new mindset is given here.
Transformation happens as you become
holy carriers of Gospel Light.
Heart is filled with sacred oil,
so you burn brightly the fire of God lit within.
Heaven's hallelujahs echo here,

and your song of praise joins in,
so every realm is filled with radiant Beauty.
This is the place of completion,
of revelation, of restoration...
a healing center where true wholeness springs up.
Some things whispered here are
just between you and the Lord,
given to ponder and build soul...
yet what happens there cannot help but
flow out into your life,
as Spirit and Truth root deep and
become who you are.

He who dwells in the Secret Place of the
Most High shall abide under the shadow
of the Almighty. Psalm 91:1
In the secret place of His tabernacle He
shall hide me.... Psalm 27:5b
You are complete in Him. Colossians 2:10

Hebrew definition of Secret...Concealed
from view, where treasures are stored,
hiding place for protection. **Thank**
You, Lord.

So Thankful

Father, I sit before You as
Holy Spirit wells up within my core,
and I am so thankful.
Mercy has met me at every twist and turn,
and has, as You promised,
turned deepest trauma to highest good.
Your Presence has filled and
Your Word has quickened,
and together they have led step
by step
by step
out of dreadful darkness into
gorgeous, healing light.
All You have ever whispered,
You have brought to pass.
Faith, then, is stirred for the yet-to-be,
the hope and marvelous expectation of
Your outpouring,

Your hand weaving divine into routine,
Your surprises of joy that
erupt when least expected.
I am so thankful, Father, to be Your child.
The blessing and honor of that position are
more than I comprehend.
Settle my heart in Your goodness, my dear Father.
This adopted one sits before You in wonder.

> *I will praise You, O Lord, with my whole heart; I will tell of all Your marvelous works. I will be glad and rejoice in You; I will sing praise to Your Name, O Most High. Psalm 9:1-2*

> *But as many as received Him, to them He gave the right to become children of God, to those who believe in His Name. John 1:12*

Sacred Hallelujah

Your Presence spreads out and fills my core,
and I can barely speak, Father.
Where are words to respond except sacred *Hallelujah*?
What suffices besides an awe filled *Thank You,
dear King*?
My soul is as an empty balloon,
that when filled with Your living Breath soars high,
with great joy and
deep delight.
Grace has overtaken me,
Love has saturated heart, and
Destiny has designed a marvelous plan of
Kingdom strength that will
move and work to restore all.
Glory.
Hallelujah.
Holy, holy, holy.
My heart yearns for highest utterances of
Praise, my Lord,

to perfume Your marvelous Throne Room.
Take my earthly hallelujah, then, and
translate it to the language of heaven.
Endless, sacred Hallelujahs –
pour forth from my root and core.
And let every moment of my life be filled with
Your holy breath.

And I heard, as it were, the voice of a
great multitude,
as the sound of many waters and as the
sound of mighty thundering, saying,
"Alleluia! For the Lord God Omnipotent
reigns! Let us be glad and rejoice
and give Him glory...". Revelation 19:6-7a

The Asking

Beautiful invitation to ask,
I am so grateful for you.
"...ask, and you will receive,
that your joy may be full."
Powerful is the call for the Most High to
overtake our circumstances,
desires, hopes, dreams,
heartaches and desperations,
to do divine works He alone is capable of-
answers man cannot bring.
Unseen realm of heaven ministering in
unseen realm of you.
Interventions released that bring
wonder and great rejoicing as "It is done!"
is the response to your poured out soul.
Amazing, that grace of His.
Astounding to be heard in Heaven's courts,
through the power of His holy Blood.

And the accomplishments that come through
the asking
will change the world.
Your world,
and beyond.

"Ask, and you will receive, that your joy
may be full." John 16:24

"Ask, and it will be given to you; seek,
and you will find;
knock, and it will be opened to you."
Matthew 7:7

Kingdom Come

Your Kingdom come, Lord.
Your Truth in our realm,
hungered for, walked in,
delighting souls and
releasing great power.
Your Beauty upon us,
and the works of our hands established.
Your great love flooding hearts,
and pouring out to others.
No kingdom prospering but Yours,
no darkness finding entrance before
the blinding light of Your Presence...
light that quickens our core,
shields on every side,
and makes clear the path before us.
Kingdom feet
carrying Kingdom heart
doing mighty Kingdom works.

Whole,
and giving wholeness.

> *"Your Kingdom come, Your will be done*
> *on earth as it is in heaven." Matthew 6:10*

> *"But seek first the Kingdom of God and*
> *His righteousness, and all these things*
> *shall be added to you." Matthew 6:33*

Abide

"Abide in Me, and I in you."
What a wonder that the King invites you
to change your heart's dwelling,
to shift from one realm to the next,
to be transformed from flesh mind and intent
to the divine,
to be thoroughly renewed as you experience the
beautiful pleasure of Holy Spirit within-
opening eyes,
unclogging ears, and
revealing marvelous mysteries of great Truth.
Holy, holy, holy is He and
thorough is His good work in you.
Abide in Him.
Stay in the place of interaction.
Settle in to life with the King.
Make yourself at home,
and get used to new realms of joy...

joy that is birthed in Spirit,
that starts in core and bubbles up into
a consuming, beautiful state of being.
The kind that radiates and changes your atmosphere,
that trusts the Lord, and looks forward to
His promises coming to pass.
Joy unspeakable, full of glory,
spilling out from the place of abiding
in the presence of the Most High.

"Abide in Me, and I in you. As the branch
cannot bear fruit of itself,
unless it abides in the vine, neither can
you, unless you abide in Me." John 15:4

But the fruit of the Spirit is love, joy,
peace, longsuffering, kindness,
goodness, faithfulness, gentleness,
self-control. Galatians 5:22

Angels Attend

Anointed of God, *angels attend you*.
Flaming arrows are caught, extinguished,
broken and thrown down
as they fiercely protect you.
Such joy is released as they
sing praise along with you!
Such strength is manifest as they
operate according to My Word,
released through your mouth!
Oh, how many times they have assisted you and
fought for you in the unseen!
And many are being released even today
on your behalf.
Greater is He that is in you
than he that is in the world,
and great are the ones
who attend you!

For He shall give His angels charge over
you, to keep you in all your ways.
In their hands they shall bear you up,
lest you dash your foot against a stone.
Psalm 91:11

...then the Lord opened the eyes of the
young man, and he saw. And behold,
the mountain was full of horses and char-
iots of fire around Elisha. 2 Kings 6:17b

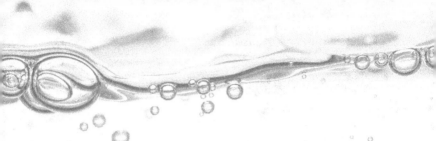

Worship

Father, I come into the place of beautiful worship,
of holy transactions,
of matchless strength and power,
of Love manifested in every molecule,
and I bow in awe.
I gather all I am to worship and honor You.
Your Spirit quickens,
and I am revived.
Your hand touches,
and I am made whole.
Your Blood covers and speaks,
and I am made utterly pure.
Your Words spoken and echoed here
form reality.
Light from Your being dances around me,
and ignites holy flame within.
Secret Place of the Most High,
shelter of Your glorious shadow...

thank You for entrance, Father,
into Your glory.
Let the joy of it flood my soul,
heal my body,
direct my spirit,
and build beautiful, magnificent Kingdom here,
in this place You created for us to dwell.

> *Oh come, let us worship and bow down;*
> *let us kneel before the Lord our Maker.*
> *Psalm 95:6*
>
> *Give unto the Lord the glory*
> *due His Name;*
> *worship the Lord in the beauty of holi-*
> *ness. Psalm 29:2*

You Alone

I come into Your Presence, Father,
and gather Truth around my soul as a
beautiful cover and mighty shield.
I cling to Your Words scripted and quickened,
and I take them into my own life.
You alone have the Words of life.
You alone see deepest core and have
the only soothing balm.
You alone bear beautiful fruits within that
cause us to rise up whole, healed,
able to reproduce Kingdom.
Bless Your holy Name!
Glory to the King of Kings!
Hallelujah to the Lamb of God,
slain for even me.
I take the power and fullness of Your holy Blood and
raise its matchless strength against every lie,
every attack of body and soul,

every generational iniquity,
every affliction in every realm.
You are victory,
Your Name is power,
Your Names describe Your great flow of mercy.
Let the fullness of all Your Blood obtained
become the fullness of all my life.

> *But Simon Peter answered Him, "Lord,*
> *to whom shall we go?*
> *You have the words of eternal*
> *life." John 6:68*

> *For in Him dwells all the fullness of the*
> *Godhead bodily,*
> *and you are complete in Him, who is the*
> *head of all*
> *principality and power. Colossians 2:9-10*

Answers

Oh, the beauty of answered prayer,
of answers that can only be
attributed to a work of God.
Such wonder,
knowing the King of Kings
truly sees your every detail,
and with great mercy and compassion
touches every part of you.
Love that cannot find words.
Mysteries too great for finite minds.
So, Father,
receive my simple, but full, praise,
and let it perfume Your courts
with the precious fragrance of
a grateful heart.

I waited patiently for the Lord; and He inclined to me,
and heard my cry. He also brought me up out of a horrible pit,
out of the miry clay, and set my feet upon a rock, and
established my steps. He has put a new song in my mouth- praise to
our God; many will see it and fear, and will trust in the Lord. Psalm 40:1-3

Again

Oh, Father.
Send Your Word fresh again,
powerful again,
with great and tender mercy once more.
I am utterly dependent on You,
and desperate for Your touch.
In this.
Again.
In what I thought was healed,
stirred with old pain.
In what I thought I had forgiven,
feeling flesh rise.
Help me, Lord.
No one else has the words of life,
the healing balm,
the restoration and joy.
I bow again.
Pour out again, Father, from Your great love.

Again

Speak.
Send Your Word to body, soul, and spirit.
Thrill me with Your manifest Presence,
Your quickened answers,
Your lovingkindness and
tender mercy.
You are so, so good,
Your mercy endures forever,
and I need it to flood my soul again.
Let healing, in every way, pour out,
and let joy and celebration arise.

> *He sent His Word and healed them,*
> *and delivered them from their destruc-*
> *tions. Psalm 107:20*
>
> *"...speak, for Your servant hears." 1*
> *Samuel 3:10b*
>
> *For the Lord is good; His mercy is*
> *everlasting,*
> *and His truth endures to all generations.*
> *Psalm 100:5*

Warfare Praise

In the midst of battle,
PRAISE.
Praise, child, is the beautiful strategy.
It cleanses and changes the atmosphere
in and around you.
It shifts focus to My strength,
My beauty,
My utter goodness.
I inhabit it,
and enemy flees it.
Angels join in as its sweetness
fills your heart and
perfumes My throne.
My Spirit quickens and soars within as
your soul magnifies My Name.
Powerful weapon,
most effective strategy,
glorious in strength!

Your praise joins and echoes the
continual celebration around My throne,
and brings heaven to earth.
And when heaven is released,
miracles happen.

> *And when he had consulted with the*
> *people, he appointed those who should*
> *sing to the Lord, and who should praise*
> *the beauty of holiness, as they went out*
> *before the army and were saying, "Praise*
> *the Lord, for His mercy endures forever."*
> *2 Chronicles 20:21*

> *But at midnight Paul and Silas were*
> *praying and singing hymns to God, and*
> *the prisoners were listening to them.*
> *Suddenly there was a great earthquake,*
> *so that the foundations of the prison*
> *were shaken; and immediately all the*
> *doors were opened and everyone's*
> *chains were loosed. Acts 16:25-26*

> *Let the high praise of God be in*
> *their mouth,*
> *and a two-edged sword in their hand.*
> *Psalm 149:6*

Poised to Produce

The Word of God is *poised to produce.*
It stands ready to flood your soul,
cleanse your core,
quicken your spirit,
and produce a beautiful Kingdom harvest
full of supernatural strength.
What a privilege to be invited to abide in the divine,
to be offered Living Words full of Living Water,
to be saturated with its grace and
washed with its love.
What a beautiful vehicle for
the very voice of the Most High to speak through,
words of God formed into words of men,
powerful, mighty, sharp and strong,
offered to all who will receive.
The overruling, overcoming, forever established Word
placed as Sword in hand,
as blazing Light for all that is to come,

as joy and celebration bursting from depths,
as peace that bathes soul.
Word of God, speak,
and produce all your fullness
in even me.

For the Word of God is living and pow-
erful, and sharper than any two-edged
sword, piercing even to the division of
soul and spirit, and of joints and marrow,
and is a discerner of the thoughts and
intents of the heart. Hebrews 4:12

How sweet are Your words to my taste,
sweeter than honey to my mouth!
Psalm 119:103

He sent His Word and healed them,
and delivered them from their destruc-
tions. Psalm 107:20

A *Mother's Heart*

Feeding of the 5000- John 6:1-14

There is an unseen character in this account, the Mom who packed her young son a little lunch to take with him to go hear Jesus. Her faithfulness and tender care positioned her child to meet with the King of Kings, and to see an astounding miracle unfold before his eyes *that included him.* And not only was he blessed to be used of God that day, but his life is forever penned in Holy Script.

Imagine him the rest of his life, retelling every detail from the perspective of a wide-eyed young boy who was eyewitness to the gracious, miraculous abundance of the Savior.

I'm sure that account became a legacy through his lineage…*because a mother was faithful to send him to hear the Word of the Master.*

I wonder what her instructions were as she sent him. *"Bring us word of Him, what He spoke, what He did. Perhaps He is truly the Christ! He is close, you must go hear Him!*

And, oh, what a report he brought home that night! We aren't told, but I would guess all those connected to the child *believed Messiah had come.*

A mother's heart became the birthplace of the miraculous.

And this mother has given her own children the bits of bread and meat that I could, and urged them to go meet the King and hear for themselves. To experience His goodness, and let their lives be penned in the Lamb's Book of Life. To take the little sustenance I could provide, and in His Presence watch it be multiplied to supply not only their own lives, but those around them.

Please, Father, bless the offerings of mothers, and multiply it greatly in the next generation.
We, too, are hungry.

Armored

The armor of God surely does something in the
Spirit realm
unseen to our eyes,
but manifested in our circumstances.
Faith protecting, deflecting,
bringing answers and victory.
Righteousness of Christ allowing no partnering with,
or opening door to,
the enemy of our souls.
Peace soothing our path.
Salvation's joy renewing our strength.
His Presence in prayer restoring our soul.
Sword of Truth tearing down lies before they take root,
cutting away deceptions and
allowing healing to flourish.
Living Water, alive in you,
refreshing heart.
Christ, who Himself is your armor,
in you.

Glory's very hope residing in
vessel of clay,
filling soul,
protecting call and purpose,
and shielding your very life.

Finally, my brethren, be strong in the
Lord and in the power of His might.
Put on the whole armor of God, that you
may be able to stand against the wiles of
the devil. Ephesians 6:10-11

Rebuild

Rebuild the ancient ruins, Father,
the places long devastated,
the desolations that have reached far,
the hearts broken,
and the rubble left behind.
Rebuild, Father,
in latter glory.
Rebuild with what never was,
with wholeness and prosperity,
with the beauty of Your Presence,
the purity of Your Blood,
the passion and love of Your perfect heart.
Rebuild in power,
in love,
in soundness of mind.
Raise walls of Salvation,
open gates of praise,
place hedge of fire, blazing holy.

Cleanse our temples in every way,
and let every part radiate the knowledge of You.
Let blessing and mercy overtake us,
let Your Word dwell in our deepest core,
and let all we are
become everything You originally intended.

And they shall rebuild the old ruins, they shall raise up the former desolations, and they shall repair the ruined cities, the desolations of many generations. Isaiah 61:4

"The glory of this latter temple shall be greater than the former," says the Lord of Hosts. "And in this place I will give peace," says the Lord of Hosts. Haggai 2:9

Violence shall no longer be heard in your land, neither wasting nor destruction within your borders; but you shall call your walls Salvation, and your gates Praise. Isaiah 60:18

Coming To *Pass*

Am I true to My Word, child?
Does My Word ever ring hollow,
and fail?
Let My word be continually before you,
renewing, planting, transforming,
bearing fruit,
exploding as fire in your bones.
It is truth.
It will bring you what you never imagined.
The Word is a Person.
The Word became flesh,
beautiful Jesus, the Christ,
son of the Living God,
Redeemer, Deliverer,
Savior, Friend.
Focus, set your gaze on Him,
and watch what will happen!
Beauty is coming forth.

Dreams and visions are becoming reality.
The Word is rebuilding ancient ruins,
creating Kingdom,
here in you.
Living, active Word...
actively living in you.

> *"So shall My Word be that goes forth*
> *from My mouth;*
> *it shall not return to Me void, but it shall*
> *accomplish what I please,*
> *and it shall prosper in the thing for*
> *which I sent it." Isaiah 55:11*

> *And the Word became flesh and dwelt*
> *among us, and we beheld His glory,*
> *the glory as of the only begotten of the*
> *Father, full of grace and truth. John 1:14*

> *For the Word of God is living and pow-*
> *erful.... Hebrews 4:12a*

Only Believe

Such great power is released, love,
as you *only believe.*
Answers wait in heaven's wings,
full of blessing and mercy,
and as you align with My Word, and
let it root in deepest crevice of heart,
faith's mighty strength begins to work wonders,
miracles,
even far above your asking.
Have I overlooked your cries, love?
Am I not forever for you,
always with you?
Security and confidence in what I have
spoken and promised,
even to you,
is not pride, love.
It is rooted, grounded, measureless
love in action.

Only believe...
Your Father so loves you.
Your King has crowned you His heir.
Your spirit is indwelt by His.
Greatest power that exists resides in you.
Believe,
and watch the works unfold.

> *Jesus said to him, "If you can believe,*
> *all things are possible to him who*
> *believes." Mark 9:23*

> *Jesus said to her, "Did I not say to you*
> *that if you would believe*
> *you would see the glory of God?"*
> *John 11:40*

> *"...He who is in you is greater than he*
> *who is in the world." 1 John 4:4*

The Presence

Through the Blood of Christ,
welcome to the Presence of God.
Beauty beyond imagining,
astounding glory and power,
a place to stand,
a place to sit.
Holy impartations,
magnificent wonders,
Word revealed.
How can mind wrap around the
stunning display?
And not only are you invited to enter,
but to *abide.*
Dwell.
So, Father, because of Jesus,
I enter in.
Cleanse me fresh,
anoint with power,
plant Your beautiful Kingdom plans.

Beyond the Veil,
soul is free to dream.
Identity secured,
gifts quickened,
flame of Spirit fanned.

Thank You, Jesus, for coming to us, and giving us by Your Blood access to the highest realm, the very Holy of Holies, the indescribable Presence of God. In that place the outpouring fills, floods, overflows earth boundaries and finite minds, and opens hearts to receive measures of Divine never imagined. Thank You, Messiah, Redeemer, Holy One of Israel who has given the sacrifice for the souls of all who will receive. I bow. I worship You alone.

This is the most beautiful place on earth, because it is NOT OF the earth. And from that place comes the most beautiful fruit.

> *This hope we have as an anchor of the soul, both sure and steadfast, and which enters the Presence behind the veil, where the forerunner has entered for us, even Jesus, having become High Priest forever in the order of Melchizedek. Hebrews 6:19-20*

> *"Abide in Me, and I in you. As the branch cannot bear fruit of itself,*

> *unless it abides in the vine, neither can you, unless you abide in Me." John 15:4*

Drink

Come to the Waters, love.
Drink deeply,
fully quenching every canyon yearning,
every dry ache,
every longing and desire.
Sweet, sweet healing waters.
The deeper you drink,
the greater your stature as you
truly rise,
truly shine,
truly become who you really are.
You will never be whole,
or wholly you,
until you drink.
Living Water nourishes your core,
nurturing the very essence of
who you were specifically and carefully crafted to be,
the essence breathed into you by Father.

392

And as you drink in life itself,
life will spring forth around you.

> "If anyone thirsts, let him come to Me
> and drink. He who believes in Me,
> as the Scripture has said, out of his
> heart will flow rivers of living water."
> John 7:37b-38

> Everyone who thirsts, come to the
> waters.... Isaiah 55:1a

> And the Spirit and the Bride say, "Come!"
> And let him who hears say, "Come!"
> And let him who thirsts come. Whoever
> desires, let him drink of the water of
> life freely. Rev.22:17

Arise, Shine

The Light that floods heaven and
causes there to be no need for sun or lamp,
is the same Light that fills your deepest core.
Same glorious radiance.
Same energy, power,
strength, warmth.
You, too, shine the Beauty of the King.
You, too, are a carrier of Glory.
You, too, are filled with supernatural rays.
Moses' face shone from The Presence.
Stephen's face glowed with glory's reflection.
You, too, love,
blaze with Light you do not realize.
Arise, shine,
for your Light has surely,
surely come!

Arise, shine; for your light has come!
And the glory of the Lord is risen upon
you. Isaiah 60:1

The city had no need of the sun or of the
moon to shine in it,
for the glory of God illuminated it. The
Lamb is its light. Rev. 21:23

...Moses did not know that the skin of his
face shone.... Exodus 34:29

And all who sat in the council, looking
steadfastly at him,
saw his face as the face of an
angel. Acts 6:15

Come

The King of Kings and Lord of Lords,
the mighty, majestic, magnificent Most High,
has given the Blood Sacrifice on your behalf and
has opened the Door,
the portal into the highest heaven,
the glorious, vibrant,
indescribable dwelling of the Master,
Lord God Almighty, Yahweh…
and beckons, "Come."
Holy Spirit says, "Come."
Father anticipates fellowship with eagerness,
and says, "Come to the throne of God!"
The very dwelling of your Father.

It is no small thing.
It is no religious ritual.

Holy Blood rebirths you into a new reality.
Light is planted as holy seed in your core,

and expands through your expression.

Holy, holy, holy is the Lord God Almighty!
Before You, Lord, my speech ceases and
my knees bow,
and the only cry found is
"Worthy is the Lamb!"

And the Spirit and the bride say, "Come!"
And let him who hears say, "Come!"
Revelation 22:17a

Then Jesus said to them again, "Most
assuredly, I say to you,
I am the door of the sheep." John 10:7

"Worthy is the Lamb who was slain to
receive power and
riches and wisdom, and strength and
honor and glory and blessing!" Rev. 5:12

My prayer for you...

I am sitting by the ocean as I type these last lines. As I look out on its magnificent depth and beauty, another part of Habakkuk 2 comes to mind:

> *"For the earth will be filled with the knowledge of the glory of the Lord, as the waters cover the sea." Habakkuk 2:14*

I truly pray that the simple words the Lord has whispered to my heart as I have sought His Presence will cause you to be filled with fresh love for Him, and to run after Him yourself, in Spirit and Truth.

Be refreshed.
Be filled with the knowledge of His glory, as the waters cover the sea.

Seek Him today, friends.
He loves you so.

In His precious, matchless Name.
So be it.